BORN SOUTHERN AND RESTLESS

Emerging Writers in Creative Nonfiction

General Editor:	Lee Gutkind
Editorial Board:	Robert Atwan
	Madeleine Blais
	James Boylan
	Annie Dillard
	P. J. Dempsey
	Laurie Graham
	Tracy Kidder
	Francine Ringold
	Ilena Silverman
	Lea Simonds
	Michael P. Weber

Born

Southern

and Restless

Kat Meads

Emerging Writers in Creative Nonfiction

Duquesne
University Press
Pittsburgh, PA

This book is published by
Duquesne University Press
600 Forbes Avenue
Pittsburgh, PA 15282–0101

Library of Congress Cataloging-in-Publication Data

Meads, Kat, 1951–
   Born southern and restless / by Kat Meads.
      p. cm.
   ISBN 0–8207–0275–7 (cloth: alk. paper).—ISBN 0–8207–0276–5
   (paper: alk. paper)
   1. Meads, Kat, 1951– —Family.   2. Women poets, American—20th
   century—Biography.   3. Southern States—Social life and customs.
   I. Title.
PS3563.E172Z47 1996
811'.54—dc20
[B]   96–25366
                                                                                            CIP

Essays, in different versions, originally appeared in the following periodicals: *Blaze:* "Dora's
Version"; *CrossRoads:* "Sports: Family Style"; *Four Quarters:* "An Emily/Sylvia Pilgrimage"; *Gulf
Stream:* "Night Life" and the "Shall We Gather" section of "Standing Between God and Me";
Lynx Eye: "The Coupling and the Un"; *Lyra:* "The Confessions of Willie Mae Hall" (as "Crazy
Zelda's Crazy Nurse"); *Malcontent:* "Testing"; *The Missouri Review:* "Almost Alone in
Albuquerque," "Exchanging Forever" and "The Piracy of Acquaintance"; *New Letters Awards
Issue, 1986–87:* "Someone Else's City"; *New Southern Literary Messenger:* portions of "Water
Terrors" (as "On the River with Dubby"); *Oasis:* "Eye of the Beheld" and "Native Son"; *Palo Alto
Review:* "Falling from Grace" and "Instruction"; *Radical Teacher:* "Instruction" (Reprint);
Southern Exposure: "Duties During the Summer of 1980" (as "Duties") and "What Miss Elizabeth
Told Me About Life" (as "Miss Elizabeth"); *Southern Quarterly:* "Live, Onstage."

"Someone Else's City" received the Dorothy Church Cappon Essay Award from *New Letters.*

"Crazy Zelda's Crazy Nurse" received the Belles Lettres Award from *Lyra.*

Excerpts from "Crazy Jane on the Day of Judgment" by W. B. Yeats reprinted with the
permission of Simon & Schuster from *The Poems of W. B. Yeats: A New Edition,* edited by Richard
J. Finneran. Copyright © 1933 by Macmillan Publishing Company. Copyright © renewed 1961
by Bertha Georgie Yeats.

Excerpts from "Wuthering Heights" and "Lady Lazarus" by Sylvia Plath reprinted with the
permission of HarperCollins Publishers from *The Collected Poems/Sylvia Plath.* Poems copyright
© 1960, 1965, 1971, 1981 by the Estate of Sylvia Plath.

In a few cases, to safeguard the identities of those involved, pseudonyms have been used in
these essays.

Design by Jennifer Matesa.
This book is printed on acid-free paper.

Contents

The first time I remember anyone making fun of my Southern accent I was twenty and staying overnight in a youth hostel in Amsterdam. My mocker wasn't Dutch; she hailed from Long Island, and I didn't immediately recognize the ridicule of my speech via hers. The friend I was travelling with, sharper and quicker, immediately launched her own counter-attack, thickening the drawl with every honey-laced barb. Toward the end, I had trouble understanding all of what she said as well, but I was impressed by the defense and her regional loyalty.

Impressed, but not finally persuaded. Thereafter, for a stretch, I did my best to disguise all elongated vowels and consonants, ferreting out those "crack the window" expressions that gave away my origin.

This book is dedicated to Dubby and Dora, two who knew that a child of the South may shake the drawl but never the influence.

The Itch of Wanderlust

Consider the evidence. Continental drift. The supercontinent Pangaea breaking into the mini-supercontinents Laurasia and Gondwanaland, setting off a chain reaction of breaking and drifting at a yearly rate of one-half to two inches, a distance of some 3,000 miles after 190 million years. Slow movement, but steady—nothing to scoff at. Oceans, too, are restless. Agitating bottom water may take 2,000 years to reach the surface, but reach the surface it does. The Atlantic, the Pacific, every ocean is an ocean in motion, ceaselessly circulating. Whales migrate, birds migrate, butterflies migrate, moose migrate, bats migrate. Why, then, should humans stay put? It's unnatural; it's anti-evolutionary; it goes against the laws of the universe. Forty-three million Americans changed residences in 1994, according to the Census Bureau. But try explaining, on an individual basis, the urge to wander. It can be a hard phenomenon to dissect, harder to defend.

"You and your brother," our father, Dubby, says, amazed. "As soon as you get fifty dollars ahead, you're off again."

2 • Kat Meads

An exaggeration, but just. As adults, Craig and I—two peas in the wanderlust pod—have moved often if not always well. Over the years our relocations have caused personal and professional setbacks, personal and professional disappointments, and financial chaos. But we've yet to lose our enthusiasm for the movement and its implicit promise of change and progress. We've yet to overdose on the adrenaline rush of new territory.

Our lust for wandering continues to perplex Dubby, perfectly content to finish off on Meads land where he started. His mother, Dora, was less perplexed than exasperated by the necessity of adding another scrap of paper, listing yet another "foreign" town and zipcode, to her already jam-packed rubber band and thumb tack drawer. Informed of a pending move, she invariably barked her indignation.

"What do you want to go there for? Why don't you just come on home and settle yourself?"

I don't know how my brother responded, but I answered Dora as frankly as I could. I lacked—and still lack—the ability to "settle myself" anywhere.

"It's a big world, Grandma," I explained, ignoring her snort. Birds gotta fly, fish gotta swim, and I gotta ramble.

Unlike my cousin Linda, I was dubbed an "outside" child early on. Indoors felt too confining. Whereas Linda could curl up with a book mobile edition of *The Count of Monte Cristo* and be satisfied to sit with it in a chair all afternoon, I preferred to play in the yard, the fields and the woods past twilight. In the near-dark, the bright glow of my mother's kitchen looked like a beacon. But I never ran toward it; I strolled.

Those afternoons Linda passed on hitting flies or scouring the woods for Lady Slippers, I sulked for a bit, but I didn't pick up a book and join her. I roamed on my own.

Back then, my mother fixed the boundaries of my roaming. Viper-phobic, she wanted me within eye-range at all times, especially during the summer when cottonmouths routinely slithered across the yard. Prepared in advance, she kept a loaded rifle in the closet. Even without leaving the back steps, she could pick off reptiles hard for me to see stretched in the grass or between pine trees. "Eye-range" sounds more restrictive than it was. From the house, my mother could scan a sizable chunk of field, the nearest edge of woods, our entire yard and the bulk of Linda's. As long as I stayed marginally within those limits, as long as my mother could look up from her cleaning or baking or sewing every now and again and feel assured that I hadn't been fanged, I could create my own itineraries.

When Linda turned seven, as a present, her father built a hurricane-worthy clapboard playhouse with real blue shingles, tiny window panes and a polished hardwood floor. Uncle Carl's construction was extravagant and very fine, but it contained only one room and a small room at that. In it, I felt scrunched. Secretly I preferred my own imaginary, mobile versions. On the edge of the woods, plenty of pine straw, pine cones and felled branches to work with, I "built" my own playhouses, distinguished by elaborate floor plans. I subdivided the ground into capacious kitchens and living rooms and bedrooms and entryways, and when I grew tired of that particular arrangement, I relocated elsewhere.

Bike passion replaced playhouse passion. My brother owned a red bike, a bike he was allowed to ride all the way to Shawboro to play baseball or basketball with his friends. In a charitable mood, he'd ride me around the yard on the handlebars as our mother screeched:

"Watch out for the spokes! Keep your feet away from the spokes!"

Pedaling on grass and pine straw and oyster shells was hard enough without the cargo bouncing up and down, and Craig quickly dumped me in disgust. My bikes were inherited from a Virginian cousin: a tiny tricycle, a bigger tricycle and a two-wheeler with training wheels. Dubby took off the training wheels within a week; I preferred falling to their debilitating drag. As soon as I started school, I started collecting Lucky Star coupons. Depending on the number of sheets of Lucky Star notebook paper within the packet, the customer got a coupon worth 10, 25 or 50 stars. My short-sighted friends handed over their coupons indifferently. No one could imagine saving enough of them to win a bike, but I did: a brand new blue and white Schwinn.

I had big plans for that bike: a trip all the way to Shawboro proper and back via East Ridge Road. It took some persuasion. My mother agreed, if and only if I rode straight there and back. When I took off, she kept lookout from the driveway. From the driveway, she could see all the way down the dirt road to the macadam and make sure no vipers, slinking from the swamp to the woods or vice versa, interrupted my maiden voyage.

Getting through the sand mounds of the dirt road was tough, but once I hit East Ridge Road I flew down that flat highway to Shawboro, hair peeled back like a banana skin, thighs pumping. In that near-jet propulsion, I felt as if I'd become speed itself. Before I knew it, I'd reached Shawboro proper, the agreed-upon end of the line. A quick trip, too quick. To lengthen it, I dallied at the stop sign, chatting with Mrs. Olive Perkins in her garden and with Mr. T. B. Gregory washing his Chevrolet in front of his general store.

"You came all the way from your house?" T. B. inquired.

"All the way," I crowed, but already that distance had begun to seem minimal, impossibly short, as if it were nothing to speak of at all.

Already I was thinking: next time I ought to ride to the short cut. Or Indiantown. Or all the way to Old Trap, another county altogether.

After a slow, homebound start, my brother and I attempted to make up some of that lost wandering time with frequent transplantings, starting in our late twenties and thirties. Since then, we've accumulated addresses north, farther south, west and farther west. Most people, most of our friends, move, if they move, for higher-paying jobs, bigger houses or better school districts, but as often as not Craig and I move because we like the sound of a town's name or a description we read in a newspaper or magazine article or because we passed through the area once and decided it might be nice to return and hang around for more than a weekend. Trained to drive tractors, combines and flatbed trucks, my brother thinks nothing of driving a massive U-haul back and forth across the country. I prefer travelling lighter. Generally I yard-sale all but the truly irreplaceable and use the proceeds to furnish my next abode. As adults, my brother and I have lived once in the same town and once in side-by-side towns, but typically we're separated by many states and many miles of highway. In the ten years Craig has lived in Asheville, Ashland, Brandon, Chesapeake, Encinitas, Efland, Henderson, Key West, Las Vegas, and Wilmington, I called Albuquerque, Austerlitz, Blue Mountain, Brooklyn, Dudley, Durham, Easthampton, Gay Head, Greenfield, Hillsborough, Los Gatos, Mebane, Newburyport, Northfield, Pittsboro, Progresso, Provincetown, Saratoga, Somerville, Temecula and a few other hot and frigid spots home.

Wherever we're temporarily stationed, my brother and I return to Shawboro for the holidays, to catch up with our parents and catch them up on us, to reacquaint ourselves with our aunts and uncles, the 42 first cousins we already know and the ever-expanding number of second and third cousins coming into the world.

Invariably, on those occasions, my brother and I are asked: "So where ARE you these days exactly?"

Avoiding the philosophical ramifications of that query, Craig and I usually supply a post office location.

And the usual response to that response is:

"Is that right?"

Whatever flashes through my brother's brain during that conversational impasse, he keeps to himself, but my brain speed dials this sequence: Is it RIGHT? Who knows? It just is. For the moment, anyway. And when that moment passes, when my favorite bookstore goes out of business, or the quality of the lettuce and pears deteriorates at Craig's favorite market, or we've simply seen all we wanted to see and done all we wanted to do at that particular latitude and longitude and yearn for a change, we'll give in to the itch of wanderlust, give notice to our landlords, hand over our rented keys, arrange for an electricity shut-off, leave a forwarding address, pack up and move again.

Dora's Version

I've seen photographs of my grandmother Meads as a young woman, and she looked only somewhat striking, never beautiful. Squarish jaw, high forehead, unsmiling mouth, the entire package a bit severe for a twenty-year-old. She stood almost a foot and a half shorter than my grandfather, Jack, who photographed lean and mischievous, a smile playing off lips so thin he called them "snake lips." She posed rigidly, front and center; he offered a teasing half-profile, hands in his pockets. Pictorially they weren't an ideal match, but photographs can sometimes lie.

Did Dora lie about the dead Jack? The portrait she created of the man most of his grandchildren never knew was the product of a deep, abiding bitterness. Although she lived longer without him than with him, the fury she felt for their years together remained fresh and easily aroused. She insisted on "setting the record straight," providing his descendants with "the truth, not some prettified tale." But what we heard, what we uneasily sat and listened to, was a tale fashioned by Dora, her scarifying version of events. We had no other option; Jack's voice and version were unavailable.

Born in Weeksville, a tiny farming community south of Elizabeth City, my grandmother predated both the automobile and the airplane. She grew up riding horses and driving horse-drawn carts, and horses were the mode of transportation she preferred. She never owned a car or learned to drive one. Wasn't necessary, she said. And anything she didn't deem necessary, she didn't bother with.

As did many in the area, her father farmed, and along with other farmers' children she and her eight siblings scheduled school work around work in the fields. After the cotton and soybeans had been harvested, they attended classes for four months until the start of the next planting season. That abbreviated educational term was the best my grandmother could hope for until a letter arrived from a cousin in New Bern, unexpectedly inviting Dora to come and live with her. In New Bern, cousin Mary promised, Dora would be able to attend nine months of school every year.

At first the idea delighted my grandmother, but the delight quickly soured.

Childless cousin Mary, Dora said, "wanted a maid and I came cheap."

In addition to attending school, Dora cleaned Mary's house and prepared the household's meals. An unrelated gentleman who called himself "Uncle" John frequently dined with the two females. After the dinner hour, he and his hostess entertained each other in the parlor while Dora washed dishes, then started on her homework at the dining room table.

One evening, as Dora told it, John sent Mary upstairs on a

book hunt as a diversion. As soon as she left the parlor, he joined my grandmother in the dining room. When he showed interest in more than her school work, he was rebuffed. Again he pressed his case. Rebuffed again, he pressed harder.

"Cousin Mary knew very well what had gone on," Dora said, but ignored the dishevelment after returning downstairs.

The parlor visit resumed.

"Never mentioned a word about it, not that night or the next day or the day after that. Invited him back to dinner too, and in he came the very next weekend, cocky as you please," Dora fumed. "I despised the sight of him and soon enough I despised the sight of her."

While Dora lived in New Bern, one of her sisters back in Weeksville became gravely ill with pneumonia. Since the doctor predicted death, Dora returned home for what everyone assumed would be a funeral service. Instead her sister rallied and rather miraculously recovered. After that recovery, Dora expected to return to New Bern, resume her role in her cousin's household and finish her education. The reversal of that expectation also came as a shock. The despised cousin Mary refused to fund the trip. In Dora's absence, she had found another, cheaper maid.

In her later years my grandmother routinely turned up her nose at religion and at the religious. Once, when a do-gooder of the Lord approached her door with a basket of fruit and New Testament tracts, determined to talk God, she waved a butcher knife in his face.

"Come round again," she said, "and we'll see about those skinny fingers of yours."

And yet the scant number of joyful memories within Dora's repertoire involved playing the piano for her church, Weeksville

Methodist, as a teenager. Describing those sessions, she looked almost pleased. Then other associations intervened. The Sunday morning Jack Meads, a dapper, dashing suitor of twenty-five, took a seat among the crowd, Dora took notice.

"I might have been striking the chords of 'Love Lifted Me,'" she admitted, "but I was falling flat on my face in love."

To hear (and see) Dora Brothers perform at Weeksville Methodist, my grandfather went against a family stand. His parents had recently broken with the "inferior" Methodists when a band of travelling evangelists passed through, convincing them God favored the Sanctified, Pure and Holy above all other sects. Large numbers of the Meads clan, my second, third and fourth cousins, still live in and around Weeksville, shunning personal decoration, playing cards and waltzes around the dance floor on religious principle. My first cousin Linda and I were introduced to that branch of the family at a fiftieth wedding celebration featuring weak punch and no dancing. Teenagers at the time, Linda and I arrived in bright lipstick, circus rouge and globs of pancake makeup. We startled our more devout relations, and they startled us. They thought Linda and I looked like harlots; we thought they looked like ghosts.

My great-grandfather fervently embraced the Sanctified, Pure and Holy cause and took up the call to join the travelling evangelists "on the spot," Dora reported. Converted, packed his bags, kissed his family goodbye and hit the road, never to be seen or heard from again. That development might have turned my great-grandmother, the deserted wife, against her new faith but didn't. For the rest of her life, she held fast to the Sanctified, Pure and Holy ways, demanding the same of her children. The day she remarried—seven years after the desertion, the first day the law allowed—she required her new husband to become Sanctified, Pure and Holy as well. With husband number two, she produced seven children, bringing her grand total to eleven. Nevertheless, according to Dora, of all her offspring my great-grandmother remained sweetest on her fourth child and first son, Jack.

A year after the favored Jack and Dora met at Weeksville Methodist Church, they married. As a bride of nineteen, Dora moved her residence five miles west to a Sanctified, Pure and Holy home in Meadstown—a crossroads so dense with Meadses any other title would have been misleading. With the exception of those two years in New Bern, she had lived solely with her parents. Her new housemate, her mother-in-law, didn't force her to change her religion *per se*, but Dora was forbidden to play the piano for the Methodist congregation. As the second husband had done, Dora also acquiesced—but not with grace and not without a festering resentment. In her personal triumvirate of evil, my grandfather was flanked by Marys: cousin Mary and Mary the mother-in-law.

"I had to live with her ordering me to do this, do that. 'Jack likes things this way, Jack wants that' and him never lifting a finger."

How, in money-poor circumstances, my grandfather got away with not lifting a finger is explained this way: "He didn't have to work, he said, because his ship was about to come in—the ship carrying the money Papa promised me in his will. Right then I swore Jack Meads would never touch a penny of it. Not the first red cent."

If you believe Dora's version, before their first wedding anniversary, my grandfather became culpable of worse than laziness. If you believe Dora, the dapper and dashing suitor turned vain and cunningly cruel.

"He told his family I was nothing but a tramp. That he'd had his way with me from the start, but since he was a gentleman, he'd married me. They believed the lie, every last one of them. Gave them another excuse to treat me like dirt. Like something not fit to wipe their boots on."

Despite his reputation for sloth and the money shortage, somehow my grandfather acquired an operating farm in Shawboro, twenty miles from Meadstown. After seven years of cohabiting with Mary the mother-in-law, Dora broke free of the meddling and surveillance and escaped by wagon at dawn. The relocation caravan included obliging neighbors, four children (aged two months to six years), horses, livestock, the family dog, hay fodder and corn for spring planting. Near sundown they reached Shawboro, a community whose houses, Dora said, "you could count on one hand."

What greeted them besides a different community and residence was more work. In Shawboro they had no kin and their children were still too young to provide much help. Meals, clothes, chickens, cows, gardens, fields. To take care of all those chores required sixteen to eighteen hours of steady labor.

"Nobody who put in a good day's work wanted anything but sleep," Dora maintained, equating sexual desire and shiftlessness, a bias of the times or a very personal assessment of her own disintegrating marriage. "After slaving all day, I had to put up with him on me half the night."

When she began to menstruate biweekly she wrote to a mail-order doctor who advertised his practice on the back page of a farm journal. To regulate her flow, Dora was advised to place a pan of cold water under her side of the bed. Dutifully she filled the pan night after night, an isolated, depressed farmer's wife, hoping for a water cure.

Four more children were born before my grandfather's death in 1944, and the seven who survive dispute Dora's version of the marriage, of Jack and of her deep unhappiness with him. They recount his jokes, his pranks, his clowning. When my Uncle Maurice was courting my Aunt Madeline, every Saturday my grandfather and his sons strung a piece of wire across the threshold to trip her suitor.

"Never learned to pick up those feet," my father and uncles howl to this day.

Jack's daughters usually describe his infinite patience, how much he loved his family, his animals and the farming life.

Perhaps in a case unconnected with bloodline I could more adamantly and with a clearer conscience side with the woman.

Perhaps not.

For the last two years of his life, my grandfather lay in a second-story bedroom, cancer's invalid, his flesh rotting from ear to collarbone. It was, by all accounts, a prolonged and terrible end.

His children, her children, all deny it, but Dora remembered standing over that death bed, calling her husband a worthless cheat, hoping aloud he'd burn in hell for the years of misery he'd caused her.

Did she remember his response? If so, she refused to say.

Neighbors
vs.
Kin

During my childhood, up our dirt road, North Carolina State Road #1204, there were three residences: the "original" farmhouse, where Dora and Jack lived after their move from Meadstown; my parents' four-room house, built by my father and Jack in the thirties; and Dora's green and silver trailer, rolled in sometime during the fifties after she deeded the farmhouse to her youngest son, Carl, his wife and five kids.

All those grandkids and their commotion had begun to play on Dora's nerves. She wanted to live alone and arranged it, ignoring the doctor's advice, downplaying her unreliable heart, and refusing to move in with any of her other children. Adamant, dogged and stubborn, Dora knew what she wanted and where: a one-bedroom mobile home, situated between the farmhouse and our house. Argued out, her children eventually gave up and gave in.

Having already created a jungle around her former residence, Dora set about surrounding the trailer with masses of forsythia, pyracantha and crepe myrtle bushes, purple, red, pink and white azaleas, jonquil and narcissus bulbs and roses of every hue. The greenery grew up thick and healthy, cocooning the trailer with fairly impenetrable vines and leaves, but still she lived only half a field from our house. When I was a teenager, playing the same 45 incessantly, the racket infuriated her. On a regular basis, she stomped over to complain.

"Do you have to play that thing so loud? You can hear it clear to Shawboro."

Moonily addicted to "Party Lights" or "The Locomotion" or some other snappy/sappy hit of the week, I thought the volume was already so terrifically subdued it verged on rock and roll heresy. But I was young then, unseasoned in the politics and niceties of the neighbor contract, my ignorance environmentally imposed. What did I know about dealing with neighbors? My neighbors were my kin.

Up Meads Lane, we took it for granted that doors went un-locked; that unannounced visits were part of the routine, early morning through late night. All of us wandered in and out of the two houses and Dora's trailer—sometimes for a reason, some-times just bored and browsing, but always without invitation. Since when do relatives need an invitation? When the need or spirit hit, you just ambled over. In my case, say, to play hopscotch or jacks with Linda. In my mother's case, to borrow some canning lids from Linda's mom, Aleeta. In Uncle Carl's case, because he needed a saw or hatchet from my father. In Dora's case because she was "give out" from all that weeding and planting and needed a break. Nonchalantly, with not the slightest twinge of embarrass-ment or apology, we burst into one another's homes during meals, television programs, baths and arguments. We pulled up a chair and ate along, watched the television program too, or simply waited for the ablutions to end. No one told anyone to come back later. That would have been rude. Moreover, it would have assumed a right of privacy. We weren't just neighbors, we were family! Privacy didn't exist.

Even so, Dora's drop-bys often took my mother by surprise. "Your mother creeps!" my mother whined to my father, who shrugged.

Dora walked softly and very slowly, but I always heard and recognized her step—deliberate, measured and easily distinguished from Aunt Aleeta's frantic pitter-patter, Linda's springy bounce or the resounding thud of Uncle Carl's tread. If I sat in the living room, I looked toward the hallway for my grandmother's emerging head. Intent on hemming the skirt of a dress or finishing a letter, my mother did not. When she did glance up and notice her mother-in-law, she generally yelped, evoking Dora's scorn.

"What are you always so SCARED about?"

"You," my mother might have answered, but never did—aloud.

When Dora still lived with her kin, the land between the farmhouse and my parents' house was cultivated. For maybe an hour after tilling, the field rows resembled normal field rows, but thereafter a pathway appeared, the soil packed and flattened by all the foot traffic crossing and re-crossing between houses.

A ditch divided the field from Linda's yard, crossed by three sagging planks wedged bank to bank. For years that rickety bridge served as a meeting place for Linda and me in actuality and in fantasy. We intersected there for tree climbing expeditions and woods explorations, and planned to meet there, midnight, whenever we schemed to run away. We often schemed to run away, as payback for inadequate dessert portions, severely early bedtimes, and the imposition of a zillion other rules and regulations we deemed unjust. Revenge primarily motivated our schemes, but we also craved a grand adventure. For sustenance, we decided on ketchup sandwiches. I was supposed to bring the Wonder Bread; she was supposed to bring the bottle of Del Monte.

"Twelve o'clock sharp," we'd promise the afternoon before runaway night, triple swearing to meet in moonlight at the ditch bridge.

But no matter how earnestly I attempted to stay awake until midnight, eventually I fell asleep, snoozing above the flashlight, Wonder Bread and sweater I had stashed beneath the bed. I wouldn't have considered running away with anyone but Linda, and together we wouldn't have considered running anywhere except into Dora's woods. We never planned to stay away forever, just long enough for the adults to weep and wail and repent their child-provoking ways. Then we'd deign to return and hang around until another restrictive rule compelled us to punish its enforcers. Schemes and resolutions we had aplenty, but we never made it to Dora's woods at midnight; we never even made it to the bridge.

With no close neighbors, my grandparents expected their family to operate as a caretaking and entertainment unit: brothers and sisters tended younger siblings; brothers and sisters played together. The next generation—mine—continued the tradition with a cluster of cousins. Until Linda, a year older, went off to school and left me to hopscotch and jacks and tree scaling for one, our Meads cluster by and large represented my world. Then the world began to widen, bit by bit.

Because the school bus didn't come up our dirt road, Craig and Linda walked out to catch it beside our line of mailboxes on East Ridge Road. Our closest non-kin neighbors, Trim and Eva and their brood, lived on a lot catty-cornered to those mailboxes. For years I knew them only as the folks who lived on the corner, folks to wave to as my mother barreled past in our '51 Ford, coating them and their front porch with dust. But that casual acquaintance changed when the son, Billy, killed my dog. Annoyed by the barking, he had shot under a dark house and hit my Labrador. The dog managed to crawl halfway home before collapsing in the middle of the dirt road where I found him, stiff and bloody. Aware of what happened, Trim and Eva made their son apologize to me, face to face. In turn, my parents made me accept that apology—or pretend to. Trim wanted to replace the dead, irreplaceable in my eyes and in my heart. My father said no; it was an accident. Accidents happen.

To a sniffling me, Dubby said: "The boy didn't mean to kill your dog."

Because I knew my father loved the dog at least as much as I did, I knew I'd have to abide by the accident theory, and no matter how much I hated doing so, whenever I passed by, I'd still have to wave and keep up the pretense of good will. It was my first lesson in the delicate art of maintaining non-kin relations. As my parents knew and as I soon learned, Shawboro was a small place. Staying on friendly terms with the neighbors wasn't so much a matter of choice as a matter of necessity. Family didn't always provide an adequate show of force. Sometimes you had to rely on the unrelated—in good times and in bad.

Farmers, particularly, relied on neighborly neighbors. If a tractor part broke or a belt snapped on the combine and there was neither time nor funds to fix it right away, farmers shared their equipment. And when hurricanes threatened, farmers helped pick their neighbors' crops, once finished with their own. Destroyed crops meant financial hardship, even ruin. Anyone mad and holding a grudge waited to vent until the crisis had passed. Everyone relied on everyone else; they had to.

Neighborliness in the female realm typically revolved around the sick and hospitalized. If the family network were too small to provide round-the-clock "sittings," other community women took up the slack. Consigned to sterile and frightening hospital wards, people believed in the comfort of a familiar face. My mother cheerfully "sat up with" a variety of folks recovering from operations in Elizabeth City's hospital or dying slowly in their homes. Never one to covet sleep, she scarcely seemed the worse for wear after her night shift, but there were plenty of other community women who needed the full eight-hour recharge and who made the sacrifice nonetheless.

If word got out that a family was down on its luck or the victim of crippling medical bills or if a family had been burned out of its home and lost every possession, the Ruritan Club or the Woman's Club organized a fried fish supper and donated the proceeds. When death touched a family, the grief-stricken survivors didn't have to concern themselves with the preparation of food. Covered dishes, fried chickens, lemon pies, boiled hams, pots of collards, and gallons and gallons of iced tea filled their kitchens as soon as the death was publicized. Food from the kitchen of Cornie Pell, one of Shawboro's most charitable, generally arrived before the mourning wreath.

Not only did Cornie enjoy a reputation as a fine cook, she was renowned for her spotless facilities.

"You wouldn't believe that kitchen floor!" I heard one of my mother's friends exclaim. "Clean enough to eat off."

A high compliment, Southern-style.

When Cornie's husband, Edward, lost his way hunting in the swamp, the people of Shawboro rushed to repay a little of their longtime debt. While the men of the community searched for Edward, the women delivered food and consolation and shared

Cornie's vigil. After passing three nights among black bears and water moccasins and hoot owls, Edward wandered out of his own accord. He'd gotten "turned around," he said and couldn't find the road back. No harm done, but he sure could use some food. The ladies of Shawboro made sure he had plenty to choose from.

When my parents had saved enough to build an extension that included two new bedrooms, one of them my very own, neighbors helped with the roofing and framing. And when another family near the short cut built a brick house from scratch, Dubby helped with that construction. My entire family helped transfer their clothes and furniture and dishes and knickknacks out of the crumbling farmhouse they left behind.

Although my mother is a terrifically talented and meticulous seamstress, she sometimes needed help with a complicated pattern or convoluted stitch. Then off we went to Miss Jenny's house. Miss Jenny sewed for most of the community, working out of her home in a side room piled high with cotton and wool and taffeta material, thread, buttons, zippers, finished and near-finished dresses, pinafores and suits. We always found her at her push-pedal Singer, a tape measure draped across her shoulders. She must have held that position fourteen hours a day. A consummate professional with forty years' experience, Miss Jenny either knew what my mother didn't or fairly quickly figured it out. And she never charged a dime for sharing the solution.

In her sixties by then, Miss Jenny understood she would live in Shawboro as long as she did live, and my mother assumed the same for herself. In the years ahead, they might need each other's assistance in matters completely unrelated to needle and thread. Failure to act neighborly held no percentage. In fact, such behavior posed a definite risk. In a small community neighborliness functioned as a kind of insurance policy wherein residents swore a reciprocal pledge: "I'll help you when you need it, and you'll help me." A very sensible agreement, given the limited resources. But what about those who don't reside in small communities, who don't expect to remain anywhere for the rest of their days? Neighborliness in transit is a far more muddled and confusing contract.

Living in my first apartment, I lived closer to strangers than I had to my grandmother. Regardless, there was no compelling reason for my new neighbors and me to become anything beyond strangers. Proximity meant simply proximity—a fluke. A temporary address united us, not bloodlines or common interests. Our apartments were less homes than pit stops for sleeping and grabbing the odd meal. We came and went and occasionally exchanged hellos in the hallway, depending on our moods or other preoccupations. Our interactions were always cursory, sometimes polite, sometimes not even that. The indifference bothered no one. Strangers aren't capable of giving offense. Giving or taking offense requires a deeper connection.

I first ran afoul of stranger neighbors in Dudley, Massachusetts because the couple living below me found my typing unbearable. Since I didn't work past ten or before seven, they weren't agitating for a schedule change; they wanted cessation. My blunt refusal to do so led to much nastiness. Until I moved out, whenever I typed, however long I typed, they beat on the ceiling with a broom handle or, when they were really ticked, with a hammer.

The week after I moved to South 8th Street in Brooklyn, I found a pile of turds stacked neatly outside my apartment door. I disposed of that message, never discovered who sent it and never investigated in any serious, methodical way—a sure sign I didn't really wish to know who operated the street's welcome wagon. But there was another reason I passed on tracking down the culprit. I didn't consider the search worth the effort. By then, I'd already decided my interlude in New York would be a brief one. A few months later I was gone.

In Asheville, for a time, I lived across from a well-meaning but exasperating senior citizen who didn't play by the usual apartment dweller rules. Lonely, she longed for companionship. As the closest and most likely provider around, I couldn't get in or out of my apartment without a lengthy conversation.

"Going to get the mail?" she'd ask for openers. Or: "Been shopping, have you?" Or: "Think it's going to rain today?"

Morning, noon or night, as soon as my key turned in the latch, she popped out from next door, as often as not wearing pajamas and bedroom shoes, her head lined with curlers. I felt sorry for her, but fairly quickly I felt sorrier for me. What she wanted and needed I was unprepared to give. Guilt-ridden but resolved, I resumed scanning the "Apartments for Rent" column in the newspaper. That go-around I held off signing a lease agreement until I had thoroughly checked out the tenants across the hall and verified that their personalities were at least as callous and antisocial as mine. One might assume that stipulation winnowed my options. It did not.

In California, I thought I'd circumvented the problem of personality altogether by renting, at long last, a house. No shared wood, steel, concrete, mail area or stairway; all floors, walls and ceilings mine and mine alone. Several hours after I moved in, sitting on my couch, getting a feel for the place, I heard my neighbors' front door open. Two sets of feet clomped onto the porch—clog wearers. I heard the clomping stop. I heard cushions sigh. I heard one, then both, cough, and I realized I had entered acoustical hell. Not only could I hear every syllable they spoke, I heard their breathing when they didn't speak. Sharing their porch seat and a smoke, I couldn't have heard anything they did or didn't do with greater clarity.

Sweet justice, my neighbors back in Dudley, Massachusetts would surely conclude. What goes around, comes around.

For my own enlightenment, I began to catalog all I wouldn't ask those "so near yet so far" porch-sitting neighbors to do on my behalf, and vice versa. Trading tractor parts wasn't an issue, but even if I sewed, I couldn't imagine tapping at their door and asking for a lesson in the latest smocking techniques. What if a member of their family became gravely ill and somehow I learned of that downturn? I wouldn't dare volunteer to pass the night at his or her bedside. Such an offer would be greeted with astonishment and quite possibly alarm; they'd think me nosy, morbid, presumptuous or just plain weird. A gift of food? Notoriously finicky about what they will and will not eat, true Californians would dump a casserole of corned beef hash into the garbage disposal after the first whiff. On the security front, if a burglar broke through my back window, would I scramble next door seeking assistance? Doubtful. If you don't feel comfortable asking someone to water your plants, you don't feel comfortable sharing menace or terror.

Why so standoffish? Because I have no idea how long they have lived in the house next door or how much longer they plan to live there. Myself, I'm due to fill out a mail forwarding order any day now. Maybe if I believed I'd be privy to their porch talk for another twenty-five years, some of my hesitations would dissolve, and we'd slowly and steadily work our way toward neighborliness in word and deed. As it stands, they have no long-term investment in me, nor I in them. Any good deeds we perform automatically fall in the "kindly acts between strangers" zone because after the first of the year or sooner, we'll very likely never lay eyes on one another again.

Standing
Between
God and Me

PERFORMANCE ART

In a community as small and rural as Shawboro, the church not only serves as a place of worship, it functions as a social nexus, a gossip crossroads, and a performance arena for preachers and ecstatic converts. Disappointingly for me, from the hard, unforgiving pews of Providence Baptist, I witnessed no outbursts of ecstasy, religious or secular, but I was privy to a few mesmerizing preacher performances fashioned to jump-start my soul toward salvation and everlasting life.

The congregation/audience at nearby Perkins Methodist often closed the show on its spiritual guru after a mere six-month run, unimpressed with his soul-saving skills or bored to snores with his monotonic delivery. We at Providence Baptist were kinder in our reviews, more tolerant of character and production flaws. We didn't demand brilliance each and every Sunday, only a competent showing. No obvious crib notes. No stuttering. No Bible verse mauling and preferably sermons organized around tried and true Baptist favorites: The Misery of Calvary, the Wretchedness of Hell.

The set design of Providence Baptist's pulpit stage never varied. A podium, flanked by two oversized, throne-like chairs upholstered in red. A painting, curtained in red, depicting Jesus at prayer, sweating blood in Gethsemane. The central aisle carpet was red; the felt attached to the bottom of the collection plates was red. Theatrical red for a theatrical purpose.

At 11 A.M. on the dot, the preacher emerged through a side door into the sanctuary and took a seat in the throne chair stage left, not yet the central attraction. Crammed between his appearance and twenty-minute monologue were several "build-up" scenes: the Responsive Reading, announcements regarding Wednesday night prayer service, Thursday night choir practice and the upcoming deacons' meeting, an update on the sick and hospitalized, more hymns, the choir's anthem, more prayers. Only then did the audience settle in to hear the week's "message." Only then did we give the program's star a chance to exhort, cajole and convince us of the gravity of our peril with all the dramatic gifts at his disposal. Remember, brethren, that "feeling sickly" list grew ever longer. Life was transitory and tenuous. Only heaven weighed in as accident-proof.

It wasn't an easy gig. The preacher worked without spotlights and their effective contrast, pools of darkness. On a sunlit Sunday morning, nothing seemed too terribly dreadful, not even eternal damnation. The audience of farmers and farmers' wives listened respectfully but without visible emotion while their kids squirmed, watched the clock and kicked the pews. At precisely 12 o'clock, whether the performance was stunning or merely adequate, the audience turned restless, ready to leave.

The preacher who led Providence Baptist when I counted as one of those squirmy kickers seemed vastly relieved by the arrival of the noon hour. Pale-skinned, buck-toothed and too tall for the podium, he hunched as he preached, a posture that did nothing to boost his authority. No presence, no magnetism, as the critics would say. His far brawnier replacement had a football player's wide shoulders, thick neck and big head. Physically he commanded the eye, but he had the odd habit of undercutting that advantage with a recitation of his various infirmities. How such a strapping man could be so "puny" stumped me and irritated the bulk of his parishioners.

"Never heard a man complain so much about so little," his audience sniffed.

In retrospect, I better appreciate the craftiness of that unorthodox ploy. Compared to the Almighty, even large, strapping mortals come off weak and puny. A subtle gambit, a little too subtle for Providence Baptist. By sticking with it, Preacher Wellons not only labored against mankind's sinning nature, he labored to convert a peeved audience.

Whether a preacher filled the pews with fans or hecklers mattered not in the least once revival week rolled around. A church's "regular" preacher couldn't preach revival. Baptist rule. Someone from the outside had to be brought in to stir up the same old, same old. A shouter, if at all possible. The most memorable of them raged and thundered with bulging eyes and slamming fists, a mass of fury and sweat. Of all the props, that drenching, dripping sweat was by far the most effective. If an eastern North Carolina August felt stifling, imagine the flames of hell!

A doozy of a shouter signed on for revival week the year I turned eight. A short, thick man, he had pock-marked skin and dark black hair that started out slicked back but whipped in every direction like a wind-driven whirligig once he hit his oratorical stride. A seasoned veteran of the revival circuit, he knew his stuff. Revivals were supposed to terrify and redeem simultaneously. The devil did the terrifying; God did the redeeming; and the revival preacher channeled both of those rollicking forces. Revival services had the potential to become sheer spectacle and did several nights of my eighth year. The red-carpeted aisle filled with sorry sinners desperate to repent, the equivalent of several curtain calls.

Midweek my father and I ventured to church alone. Prey to one of her migraines (brought on by the previous night's shouting, perhaps), my mother stayed behind. Had she been in attendance, I never would have been allowed to sit on the second pew with my best-friend-at-the-time JoAnn. Less suspicious of bad behavior before its outbreak, Dubby saw no harm in the seating arrangement.

We got through all the preliminary hymns and prayers just fine, JoAnn and I, feeling very smart and grown-up, sitting practically in the preacher's shadow. Maybe we fought over the hymnal a couple of times and giggled over a private joke, feet dangling and dress bows smushed, but for the most part we acted decorously—until nature called.

"I've got to pee," JoAnn whispered as the preacher revved up.

"How bad?" I whispered back.

"Real bad."

Foreseeing the consequences of that need, I went rigid with alarm. I knew about needing to pee badly and about trying hard not to need to. I also knew the miseries of "holding it in." But to get from our second pew to the facilities, we had to streak in front of the pulpit and a fiery preacher whose path I never wanted to cross literally or figuratively.

For a while, ignoring JoAnn's agitation as best I could, I sat perfectly still, hoping that if I concentrated on the sermon, in full-out fire and brimstone mode by then, JoAnn's pressing need would go away. It didn't, but very soon, goaded by the power of suggestion, I had to pee too.

We squirmed; we whispered; we debated.

"Let's just go!"

"We can't!"

"But I HAVE TO!" JoAnn moaned, holding her belly.

Glancing up, we saw the preacher's glowering eyes trained directly on us, the fidgets in the second row. Clearly infuriated by the disruption, he scowled long and hard our way. The severity of that attention was supposed to shut us up. What it did was finish off any doubts about our ability to ride out the piss tide. Terrorized, we really needed to pee.

No recourse left, hand-in-hand, heads bent low in shame, we bolted for the door. My cheeks burned with embarrassment; JoAnn's clammy hand stuck to mine. For the first few steps, blood pounding in our ears, we didn't notice the sudden, all-encompassing silence. And then we did.

It would have been nice, extremely nice, if someone, anyone, had let loose an understanding chuckle, but no one obliged. The exiling silence continued until, the focus of every eye in the place, we reached the door. Before opening it, I glanced one final time in apology and supplication toward the preacher. We were just little girls, little girls who had to pee. But the gaze that met mine showed neither humor nor compassion, nor the slightest trace of Christian charity, that much bandied-about virtue. With all our monkey business, we'd stolen the limelight, stolen his show.

Compared to an upstaged preacher, brethren, hell hath no fury.

SHALL WE GATHER

A member of Providence Baptist, a woman named Bertha, was addicted to re-dedicating her life to Christ. Arthritic and hearing-impaired but zealous, infinitely zealous, she made her painfully slow way to the front of the church every Sunday to clasp the preacher's hand and murmur in his ear.

Spellbound, sanctimonious Bertha *believed.* She believed in her piety and its eternal reward. She believed her soul would soar from the cage of an arthritic body to join its Maker. And she believed that the end of the world was nigh in 1956. Ready, eager even, for that coming apocalypse, Bertha felt certain of her ability to ferret out the Antichrist and welcomed the chance to call that impostor a liar to his face.

Many, a great many, wearied of Bertha's re-dedications, and the eighteen and under crowd openly smirked and snickered. Regardless, Bertha would not be deterred. Invariably she waited for the hymn's final chorus to initiate her approach, forcing the organist to drag out the last plaintive note, finger glued to the keyboard. At a maddening pace, she then inched her way toward the preacher, waiting patiently as he had waited so many Sundays before to take hold of her hand and listen to whatever repentance speech she had prepared. For the sake of appearances, he tried hard to convey joyful exuberance, greeting his single respondent for the day. At least there was Bertha! At least there was one! But after months of the same outcome, even he couldn't hide his disappointment. Again and again he'd done his best to persuade the hard of heart and Bertha, only Bertha, had taken to the aisle.

I suspect that underutilized aisle pleased Bertha enormously; I suspect she reveled in its undercrowding. Our apathy assured her she wouldn't have to compete too strenuously for God's attention once within the pearly gates. Prior to that ascension, however, as much as she might have preferred otherwise, she couldn't entirely neglect her Christian duty to proselytize to the lost—proselytizing to the lost was part of the contract that guaranteed her a leg up to heaven. Tellingly, she brought none of the fervor of her rededications to the "ministering" enterprise; in that area, her enthusiasm remained decidedly subdued. To my knowledge, Bertha never pressed any sinner too long and hard about his or her shortcomings. To have done so might have jeopardized her own eternal interests, you see. And Bertha vigorously protected her eternal interests.

As for me and my sinning self, Bertha didn't need to extol the joys of salvation. Early on I pursued redemption with a vengeance. Before turning six, I burned to join church and save my wretched soul. Whenever my mother and I bumped into the buck-toothed preacher, picking up his mail at the post office or swigging down a cola at the store, I pelted him with questions. Who made God? for instance.

"Well, now," he stalled, looking over my head at my mother.

"Don't you know?" I pestered—relentless, bratty.

But I was concerned, upset. If the preacher couldn't tell me, who could?

Soon thereafter I began composing "sermonettes" on **LOVE** and **THE DEVIL**, practicing my delivery before mirrors, honing my exhortations. On holidays and other special family occasions, I parked myself on a set of knees and with minimal persuasion delivered those little ditties to the room at large. My parents usually flinched, but there was always one in the crowd who applauded wildly, praising the love of God that shone through me. I liked the idea of glowing from whatever source.

For quite some time, I'd been observing Bertha's comings and goings, impressed by her grim determination to get to the preacher, inflamed joints and all. Desperate to know what she whispered and he responded, I could only wonder; my parents refused to speculate on the subject. Eventually I decided if I got to the preacher, I could improvise the script. The Sunday following that conclusion, I resolutely tried to weasel my way around my mother's arms, my father's legs and successfully beat Bertha to the draw.

I didn't make it.

Firm believers in private, silent demonstrations of faith, my parents were appalled by the intensity of my grandstanding inside of church and out. For all their disapproval, I remained fanatically adamant: I wanted to join Providence Baptist; I wanted to be saved; I wanted to accept Jesus Christ as my Savior; I wanted to dwell in the house of the Lord forever. When I continued to badger them to let me, they invited the preacher to our house for a *private* discussion.

Primed and ready, before the preacher had chance to speak, I rattled off all my Bible School and Sunday School lessons. I recited the Twenty-Third Psalm and the Lord's Prayer in full and quoted lengthy portions of my **LOVE** sermonette.

The preacher's smile was amazingly long-lived.

"Well, now," he said as soon as I took a breath.

It was a stellar performance, but the verdict went against me nonetheless. The adults huddled and among themselves decided I had plenty of time to join the church. No need to leap into the baptismal font *immediately*; my soul wasn't in the acute jeopardy I feared. Taking me aside, the preacher carefully explained an amazing Baptist escape clause. Until I turned thirteen, my sins smudged only my parents' charts. *Relax. Enjoy yourself. Be bad while you can*, he more or less counseled. The revelation of that transgression qualifier gave me pause; I'd never heard the "thirteen rule" before. When enlightened, I still had more than seven years to run amuck without penalty. Eventually I decided I might as well take advantage.

I count that home conference and its consequences a preacher misstep. As a certified soul saver, he should have snapped me up when he had the chance. Gradually my passion for God cooled, then petered out altogether. Bertha, if aware, no doubt danced a jig. All danger of my elbowing her out of the way in my rush for the preacher's hand had vanished. I had joined the ranks of the apathetic—at least until D-Day. For all my wanton, blame-exempt sinning, I never lost sight of the thirteenth-year cutoff. Officially baptized or not, I was still Baptist enough to appreciate that looming threat.

Late in my twelfth year, the church's musical director formed the first youth choir, and all my friends and I rushed to sign up. We sang every other Sunday, alternating with the adult choir, and wore bright yellow robes with black collars, sewn by our mothers. In the official group photo, we look like a flock of canaries perched on the church steps. As song birds, we had more energy than talent, but the congregation seemed to be entertained by our squalling renditions of "Do Lord" and "On the Jericho Road."

A natural target for "Won't you dedicate your life?" pleas, the youth choir provided fresh blood, so to speak. One after another my pals abandoned the choir loft to tread the carpet and clasp the preacher's hand. My cousin Linda, my friend JoAnn. Baptisms were scheduled every eight weeks and into that eighth sermon, warbling the final hymn from the choir loft, I knew I had to declare my own abounding faith if I wanted to join Linda and JoAnn at Blue Lake. Knew and still hesitated. Try as I might I couldn't feel "the touch of the Spirit," didn't hear "the call."

Even Bertha reached the preacher before I did that fateful Sunday, but eventually I got to him too, out of breath and shaky. I still hadn't figured out what I was supposed to mutter, pumping his hand.

"Go ahead," he encouraged.

"I want to join church," I choked out.

Apparently that stripped-down declaration sufficed. He didn't probe the whys and wherefores or question me further on other concerns. He squinted, nodded and released my hand.

A mere rededicator, Bertha was allowed to return to her seat, but I, as a first-time confessor, had to remain up front with the preacher while the congregation resettled and voted on my petition for membership. Tensely, I waited for objections. Some wise deacon would see through my last-minute scramble and charge me with inferior motivation. I half-expected my parents to declare I was still too young for soul-relinquishing commitment. But neither they nor anyone else rose to protest on any grounds. My request was treated as genuine, not counterfeit. The congregation of Providence Baptist voted me in.

In a nanosecond, people engulfed me.

"You will never regret this decision," someone my brother's age gushed.

People who weren't relatives wept over me. One of the eldest members of the congregation, a smoky lens hiding his missing eye, nudged my foot with his cane. *He* will be my denouncer, I thought: with his good eye he has zeroed in on my blasphemous soul. But Brother Burwell only wheezed and bent double and stroked my wrist.

"Welcome, child," he said.

It was Brother Burwell who led the a cappella singing of "Shall We Gather at the River" when JoAnn and Linda and I and the others gathered at Blue Lake—neither a river nor a lake, but a greenish watering hole for cows. Among the spectators stood Bertha, looking old and grim, dressed entirely in black, the thick heels of her sturdy shoes sunk in bank mud. Was she really scowling? I certainly thought so.

Burwell's voice wobbled on notes high and low, but the open-air chorus spiritedly sang about "the beautiful, the beautiful river," facing the cow pond and the pond's usual customers, temporarily fenced on higher ground. When I reemerged from that pond, algae-slimed and dripping, as far as the Baptists were concerned I was free and clear—set on the path of righteousness, garments white as snow, heaven-bound and hell-immune. By virtue of immersion, I could break every commandment ten times over as long as I muttered contrition with my last dying breath.

Even faced with a violent, unexpected end (gun shot to the head, stab wound to the heart) I figured I could steal from death a second's worth of regret. Another Baptist escape clause: I'm sorry/Forgive me/Okay.

SAVE ME

The hymnal used by Providence Baptist was published by the Convention Press of Nashville, Tennessee and edited by Walter Hines Sims, the secretary of the Church Music Department of the Sunday School Board of the Southern Baptist Convention. In his foreword, Mr. Sims attributed the final form to the "work of a committee of thirty-seven men and women from all sections of the Southern Baptist Convention."

Within the committee, he noted, there were subcommittees on contents, topical index, theology and tunes. All committees and subcommittees made a "genuine effort . . . to preserve the many hymns and gospel songs . . . so meaningful to the worship, education and evangelistic activities of Southern Baptists throughout the years."

All five hundred plus of them.

James Sullivan, Executive Secretary-Treasurer of the Sunday School Board, Southern Baptist Convention, contributed a preface. "Christianity," he wrote, "has progressed on the wings of song." He also pointed out that singing hymns counted as a "Christian privilege given to every redeemed soul." I must have agreed. Across the top of his preface, in a child's script, I scribbled "Sing! Sing! Sing!" followed by several Halaluja(s). Correct spelling seemed unimportant in my exalted state.

Before joining the youth choir, I sat with my parents during the preaching service, which meant I shared a hymnal with either my mother or my father. Dubby didn't sing, although my grandmother claimed, sufficiently inspired, he "sang like a saint."

I tried to incite that saintly serenade on many occasions by singing more loudly than I customarily did, nudging his elbow and other shenanigans. I thought surely I could prompt him into joining the chorus of "Bringing in the Sheaves," a farmer's anthem if ever there were one, but no. Even during that ode to the fields, Dubby kept mum.

He could have sounded like a frog instead of a saint and blended in fine with the congregation of Providence Baptist. As a whole we weren't a tuneful or rhythmic group. The singing dragged and the organist matched the singers' pace. Even those hymns written perkier than "The Old Rugged Cross" tended to sound strained and mournful coming from our throats, as if to underscore the long and arduous climb to heaven—nothing easy or perky about it.

For customer convenience, Walter Hines Sims and the Convention Press laid out the hymnal thematically, with songs grouped around such headings as *God the Father, Jesus the Son, The Holy Spirit, The Word of God, Salvation* and *The Christian Life.* Despite the number and variety of possibilities, our congregation stuck fairly close to a list of staples. In the *Jesus the Son* category, for instance, we preferred "I Have Found a Friend in Jesus," "Tell Me the Story of Jesus," "Jesus Is All the World to Me," "Jesus, Thy Boundless Love to Me" and "Jesus Loves Me." In the *God the*

Father section, we sang "Guide Me Oh Thy Great Jehovah," "He Leadeth Me" and "Teach Me to Pray." Some of the other perennial favorites included: "Abide with Me," "I Need Thee Every Hour," "On Jordan's Stormy Banks I Stand," "I Stand Amazed in the Presence," "There Is a Name I Love to Hear" and "I Know My Redeemer Liveth."

Beyond pleas for salvation and guidance and declarations of love and faith, an additional element united our standard repertoire, the I, I, I/ME, ME, ME factor. It may have appeared to be a group sing on Sunday mornings, but the arrhythmic, off-key dirges wafting skyward begged for one soul and one soul only. Our obsession with divine intercession was strictly personal.

To hell with the rest.

While the preacher sprinted toward the vestibule and positioned himself to glad-hand the homeward bound, we finished off with the Doxology, page 514. Theoretically the congregation sang with heads bowed and eyes closed. I bowed my head, but I kept my eyes open, sneaking glances at Dubby, trying to catch him trilling along with the rest of us. Maybe he just didn't like to sing in public, a simple case of reticence. Or maybe those egomaniacal SAVE ME! SAVE ME! requests annoyed him. Either way I was a child watching one of her parents resist a community load of pressure to celebrate the Lord in song.

Heresies start small, burgeon.

Water

Terrors

White settlers renamed Indiantown, Indiantown, but the natives called the area Coulon. Both groups, the originals and the usurpers, valued the creek for its access to North River. As one of North Carolina's first ports of entry, Indiantown thrived before the Norfolk Southern railroad came to Shawboro in 1881. All kinds of goods were bought and sold via water freight, and locals boarded at Indiantown for shopping trips to Elizabeth City and Norfolk. A grocery store, saw mill, cotton gin, grist mill and post office flourished at Indiantown Landing during the 1920s, but that second phase of prosperity ended with The Great Depression. Buildings, abandoned by owners who had no choice but to abandon them, rotted in the eternal dampness, some of those timbers sinking to the bottom of the creek bed, recycled as fish shelter.

Beyond the short and narrow concrete bridge suspended to the right of the landing, no man-made construction of any sort competes with the constructions of nature now. The creek and swamp have reclaimed everything. Putting the boat in at Indiantown, we put into water that looks and smells primeval: a brown gash, zigzagging its way across cypress knees and black gum roots to the sea.

Some years during July and August a type of flowering algae overruns Indiantown Creek. Its clusters advance from either bank, marooning fallen birch and maple and cedar logs, wreathing the water lilies, each plant very tiny and yellow-green. If you lean over the boat's edge and trail your fingers along the surface, the algae divides, momentarily revealing the fluid darkness beneath. Tugged at, a few of the stalks will break, but not before registering a spooky, counter-tug downward.

It takes all of July and much of August before the algae completely seals the creek, but once that happens the most alluring bait won't tempt the fish. To catch bass and speckled perch, round robin and flounder, the occasional catfish that settles on bottom, motionless as a stump, Dubby and I must travel beyond the creek, out into North River. And, even there, past eight in the morning until dusk, there's no good fishing. The sun's too hot, the water's too hot. Fish don't care for sweltering temperatures any more than most humans, but I'm a fan of bright light, the brighter the better, and my father indulges his only daughter's preference. Without complaint, he motors me, the dog, a six-pack of Pepsis, two fly rods and two bamboo poles down Indiantown Creek at midday.

I like to fish, but I like better the ride with Dubby, past hanging moss, wild roses and fallen logs that make curves out of the straightest stretches of water. During algae season there's a remote chance that the outboard will clog, forcing us to paddle back to the landing. It would be no great catastrophe, only a complication, but I exaggerate the likelihood—I always have, overly conscious of the turtles, wild rabbits, deer and deadly cottonmouths we speed by, cottonmouths so sassy they hold their ground even when doused by our wash. When the vipers aren't sunning themselves, they swim, heads skimming the surface like periscopes, their threat and danger three-quarters submerged. As late as thirty years ago, Indiantown Creek was thick with snakes, Dubby says; every fisherman carried a rifle. You never knew what might fall into your boat, and you wanted to be prepared.

As the aliens in this environment, we would seem likely targets for revenge, I think. It's a random, passing thought, but the moment I think it, our boat begins to feel too short, too shallow, too narrow, too insubstantial, too unstable. What defense does fiberglass provide against an element whose mass and depth could do us in, whose inhabitants could do us in? I call this kind of thinking "the dreads." Dubby calls it what it is: "fretting over nothing."

As the creek widens into river, we streak past the cypress grove that marks the bear reserve. Up ahead, a string of crab pots, tagged by bobbing Clorox bottles, lines the waterway. At the second egret's nest, we veer right and Dubby cuts the engine. The drift takes us to the edge of a marshy spit and we drop anchor, close enough to the Intracoastal Waterway to see the pleasure boats cruise by. As we rock in the swell of that constant traffic, the dog stares down into the dark water, primed for our first catch. Dubby, less impatient, angles his cap to cut the glare and settles in for the long haul.

Although he takes me fishing when I want to go, Dubby prefers the river in deep twilight, when whatever breeze there has been dies out and the water turns glassy. Unlike me, he doesn't need to make peace with the river; he is at peace here, someone who can fish for hours without taking a Pepsi break, who can locate round robin in an east wind, who can land bait between water lilies blooming six inches apart. With Dubby as my guide I've spotted buzzards' nests, bear tracks, bobcats and countless deer in motionless camouflage. I need the guidance. Left to my own devices, I tend to dwell on my awkward footing in the wobbly boat, the distance between it and a soggy, not entirely solid shore. In wide open water the dog and I both cower, trying to block out the fact that we're floating, merely floating, and bumpily at that.

A tidal wave broke over East Pakistan in the fall of 1970. At the Ganges Delta, in the Bay of Bengal, the ocean floor "was perfect for generating tidal waves," an account of the disaster explained. Near midnight, residents heard a rumbling that built slowly to a roar. As they peered out their windows, they thought they saw a luminous cloud hanging above the water, shining through the darkness. What they actually saw was a towering wall of water poised to crash. Nearly one million people lost their lives. For three days, six children floated in a wooden crate their grandfather had loaded them into moments before the tidal wave broke. Among the lucky ones, they were rescued, but they never saw their grandfather again.

I should have turned the page faster; by reading each and every detail of that harrowing saga, I only increased the potency of my already too potent tsunami dreams. For longer than I care to remember, my nights have been flooded with lethal, crashing, sucking water. Dream to dream, some of the minor details vary, but the basic plot is this: a gigantic curl of water rises up in the distance. I see the danger, know it's coming, but the advance warning proves useless. Since I can't outrun the force, my survival depends on how long I can hold my breath, my ability to dive through. I wait for the onslaught, the downpour, steeling myself for the crash and the initial going under. In no variation do I reach the wave's backside or escape water for air.

The Christmas my brother mentioned tidal wave nightmares (caused by holiday overeating, he reasoned), Dubby told a story I'd never heard based on an event I didn't remember. I was three years old, at the beach near the Nags Head pier, picnicking with my family and several other families. At that age I was crazy about the ocean, Dubby said, and ran for it every chance I got. That particular day, distracted by fried chicken and deviled eggs, no one noticed my mad dash for the waves until I was already in the surf and under. When my father scooped me out, I was shell-scraped and choking on salt water but otherwise okay. Even so, I spent the rest of the afternoon on a blanket beside my mother. Like me, my mother claims to remember no such incident.

I do remember going under at ten, again at Nags Head. The majority of picnickers that day had tired of water sports, but Marguerite Cartwright agreed to take a friend and me past the breaker line. As a trio we sailed over dozens of waves, before we saw it coming: a huge one, curving too early, approaching too fast. Marguerite tightened her grip and we kicked hard to rise above its crest, but it knocked us back and under anyway. During the somersault, before I understood I was being swept toward shore and not away, I fought with all my strength to keep hold of Marguerite's hand, and still the ocean worked its way between our fingers and broke us apart.

After that, all bodies of water, still or churning, spooked me. Learning to swim, I was supposed to start out with the Dead Man's Float before graduating to the breast stroke. One of our older cousins had taken on the job of teaching Linda and me water tricks in the placid waters of Tull's Bay. Linda obediently plunged forward, arms and legs stretched wide as a spider's, but I couldn't bear to float face down, hair spiraling like a halo, ears tuned to water sonics. I'd lost my water nerve.

During my baptism the following year, I had to ask the

preacher to bend the rules. Going under, I needed to hold my nose. Otherwise, I felt certain I'd choke.

The candidates for baptism were arranged along shore by height; at each gradation the preacher drifted backward and deeper into Blue Lake. Because one hand held a Bible, he couldn't use both hands to guide us under. We had to lean against his right arm, trusting it to dip us once, twice, three times: in and out.

Ahead of me, my friend JoAnn edged cautiously forward. The water rose from her ankles to her knees to the skirt of her dress, almost to her sash before she changed her mind and abruptly changed course. Immediately her mother broke from the clot of spectators, rushing past the few of us left at water's edge. Before JoAnn could step onshore, she was spun around and shoved back toward the preacher. It was a firm shove, a shove that left no room for misinterpretation or misunderstanding. The second trip into Blue Lake ruined the starch job on the rest of her dress, but once JoAnn reached the preacher's side, for all her initial misgivings, she didn't resist the descent. She crossed her arms, closed her eyes and submitted to the drop.

I thought I was being cagey, whispering my request for modifications, but sound carries well over water. To my utter humiliation, all on shore heard my nose-holding codicil. The preacher wasn't thrilled with the variation but agreed, tired of standing in the muck of Blue Lake and ready to come ashore himself perhaps. And thus in the name of the Father, the Son and the Holy Ghost I too went under in a posture slightly fetal.

I expected to dream of water, waiting for my brother's rescue off an island in the rain-swollen Haw in May of 1971, but sleep came in snatches that night and I remembered none of my dreams if I dreamed at all.

The beautiful 80-mile river flows easterly from Guilford County through the Piedmont Crescent and eventually into the Cape Fear River, but that May night a great many of us concentrated on a strip of dry land it coursed around, 200 feet upstream from a single-lane bridge on old Raleigh Road, three miles east of Pittsboro. An airlift by a helicopter crew from Seymour Johnson Air Force Base in Goldsboro was scheduled for dawn, but until then my brother and his canoeing partner, James, had to wait out the night in a snake-free tree. The Chatham County sheriff, his deputies, members of the local rescue squad, my sister-in-law and I waited in the Chatham County jail.

The Chatham Record reporter assigned the story acknowledged that canoeing down the river, especially at flood stage, had been a popular sport "as long as the oldest citizen can remember." But the frequency of the practice hadn't endeared it to the locals. Many found it foolhardy and said so. People got injured; people got killed.

There were two canoes in Craig's party, the second manned by another friend and a professor of pharmacy at UNC-Chapel Hill named Magus. The four had put in together near Bynum, but the canoes became separated during the trip downstream. When Craig and James's canoe flipped, they swam for the closer island. The other two paddled toward shore.

As *The Chatham Record* reported it, Don Augustine, North Carolina wildlife protector, came upon Magus and his partner during a routine patrol. The three established contact with Craig and James on the island, determined the stranded were relatively safe and unhurt, then set off to contact the rescue squad and the wives. When my sister-in-law, Jane, called me, it was already twilight. By the time we arrived at the bridge, the dark banks were lined with rescue workers and the curious, and the worst that would occur had.

Ignorant of that fact, we asked the first person we saw for information. Obligingly he told us a man was dead. Swept off by the currents. Drowned.

"I'm sorry," he said as Jane screamed, "but it's true. One of them is dead."

He just couldn't say which one.

What happened, according to Don Augustine, was this: Magus wanted to try to rescue Craig and James by swimming to them. "It was around 7:30," Augustine said. "The river was muddy and still rising. I told him to leave the boys over there until morning, but he wanted to try to get them off."

Unbelievable as it seems, someone else's husband and brother wasn't bodily prevented from attempting that doomed mission. Magus put on a life jacket, tied one end of a 400-foot rope around his waist, the other around a tree, and plunged into the rushing waters. Despite the turbulence, he imagined he could reach the island 150 feet away. Flashlights lit his progress, Augustine said, until Magus disappeared behind some bushes. After that the would-be rescuer didn't reappear or respond to calls.

"He must have hit his head on something or the strong current pulled him under," Augustine concluded.

For a few seconds after the flashlights lost track and the calling ceased, the rope registered resistance, observers said, then none.

I never questioned my brother about his dreams that night, or determined whether or not he could dream, crouched in a tree, hearing a chorus of voices, seeing a laser show of flashlights, then hearing and seeing nothing until morning. When he stepped from the helicopter onto good, hard, solid ground, nothing mattered except his safe return and the indisputable fact that he was alive and well and not a floating corpse, adrift downstream.

But later, when the shock wore off a little, when I could once again stand alongside bodies of water without getting the shakes, I did wonder what Craig had been thinking when his canoe first started to roll, guaranteeing him communion with the thunderous waters of the Haw. The moment he realized the inevitability of that contact, was he able to tap into his father's sense of water peace, or did he share his sister's terror, going in and going under?

Falling
from
Grace

Mrs. Lois Hooper, sixth-grade teacher at Moyock Elementary, a mother of four going on five, was a Mormon, a speed reader, a faultless enunciator, strict, fair and formidably intelligent in her maternity frocks. When she overheard too much profanity on the school grounds, she copied a threatening paragraph of difficult words onto the blackboard in her even script and encouraged us to memorize the "highbrow" curse.

"If you have the audacity to doubt my veracity, or even insinuate that I prevaricate," it began, ending with the teaser "medulla oblongata."

In essence: mess with me, and I'll brain you.

We were charmed. Kids who stumbled over the poetics of "Blessings on thee, little man/Barefoot boy with cheek of tan" had every syllable and comma down pat before the bus ride home. Antsy to try out our new verbal weapon, we bludgeoned our schoolmates. They were amazed, then envious. Gee, their teacher never taught them anything neat like that.

Tough cookies, we said, instantly possessive. Mrs. Hooper was *ours*.

Because her husband coached, she attended all the basketball games, but that milieu didn't fit her. Unlike other diehard fans, she didn't screech, turn blue in the face or break a sweat. She applauded when applause was called for, offered quiet congratulations if we won, then walked home across the baseball diamond to the teacherage, as it was called, a county-owned duplex built in Mt. Vernon style.

Students knew the Hoopers were Mormons without having a clear idea of what being a Mormon entailed—a shortcoming shared, I believe, by the PTA. Everyone knew they had to cross county lines to find a Church of Latter Day Saints, but precisely how they worshipped once inside remained a mystery. They never proselytized to our gaggle of Baptists and Methodists. During a weekend trip to historical points of interests, Mrs. Hooper conducted a brief, nonsectarian service based on the Book of Psalms outside a Bath farmhouse, after which we re-boarded our chartered bus and headed for the bowels of the USS North Carolina.

I considered myself a favorite; I was certainly her acolyte. I read what she suggested and accepted her stated or implied opinions. Although all of us spoke with Southern accents, various dialects competed—backwoods versus coastal and so forth. By the time we reached sixth grade our speech patterns had all but merged, but some of our parents retained their idiosyncrasies. When we mocked the idiom, Mrs. Hooper was quick to point out the progress angle. Her mother didn't speak grammatically either, but she had sacrificed to send Mrs. Hooper to school so that the next generation wouldn't continue to maul the language.

I thought we were meant to extract two morals from that

example. One: "respect your elders." Two: "respect the differences among us."

Judging by later events, I mistook the second.

When Moyock Elementary held its first spelling bee, Mrs. Hooper served as moderator. Roseanne Dale and I were the sixth grade contenders and Linda partially represented the seventh. In the cafeteria, the sun shining in at an unfamiliar afternoon slant, we lined up against the empty food bar, facing a student body seated at tables wiped clean. Called upon, we repeated the word Mrs. Hooper assigned, arduously spelled it out, repeated it again in conclusion, then waited for a judgment of correct or incorrect. With each new dropout, we bunched into a shorter, tighter, tenser line.

There were five or six of us left when I tried to spell "liveliness," spelled it L-I-V-E-L-Y-N-E-S-S, and stayed in the race. Conscious of a rustle-whisper, I thought the commotion was an echo of my own nervousness, not dissension. In the end I retired third from last, leaving Roseanne and Linda to battle out first place. For a good long time they battled, tit for tat, until Roseanne made a mistake that Linda corrected before spelling a completely different word and clinching the title.

I wanted Linda to win because she was my kin and because she had the steel nerves necessary to compete at the district level. My "nerves" were of a much flimsier sort and Roseanne's, while steadier than mine, fell victim to other pressures. Without articulating the precise nature of the home threat, I understood that she had plenty to cope with without the extra burden of a district spelling bee.

During recess following the match, several eighth graders

circled in. They wanted me to re-spell "livelyness."

I asked why, alarmed by their tone.

"Just spell it."

So I did. Again.

Wrong, they said. I should have been eliminated seventh, not third, they said. I got to stay in because I was Mrs. Hooper's pet, they said. And then they marched away.

I'm not sure which aspect of the accusation upset me more: that I had cheated or that Mrs. Hooper cheated on my behalf. Although I knew with absolute certainty she'd never break the rules for anyone, I felt horribly guilty about my role in the controversy. If I hadn't been so stupid, if I'd spelled the word correctly, she would have been spared the defamation.

Back in our classroom, waiting to board the bus for home, I tried hard not to cry. When Mrs. Hooper sought an explanation, Roseanne (seeking to be helpful) told all. I started a blubbery apology but didn't get far. In a whiplash of fury Mrs. Hooper jerked out the door and down the hallway, heading for the unsuspecting eighth grade. Both classroom doors and the transoms above them were open. We, the deserted, heard every word.

And what thunderous, wrathful words they were. If anyone had anything to say about the way she conducted the spelling bee, say it to her face. She had a cold, perhaps misheard, but neither justified an attack on one of her students. She said much more, terrifyingly eloquent in her outrage. We'd never known higher drama from any teacher, and for its violent outbreak I blamed myself.

On the bus Linda countered: "It's not like you won or anything. Roseanne came in second. If I couldn't go, they'd send her, not you."

As usual, she talked sense. But Linda hadn't been there; she hadn't been privy to Mrs. Hooper's righteous rage.

A righteous rage seemed to take possession of every adult in Currituck County the year I graduated eighth grade. It was aimed against a government that threatened to end the segregation of races, but its spillover polluted every aspect of community life. I'd like to claim that my family counted among the Southern minority who supported integration and understood the value of improved education for all, but it didn't. My relatives believed, along with their friends and pastor, in a rigid racial dichotomy. If a black worshiper dared to appear in the vestibule of Providence Baptist, the congregation, so voted, would immediately adjourn. Although its sunbeams sang "red and yellow, black and white, they are precious in His sight," the site where nonwhites were considered precious and welcome lay elsewhere.

In the county, there were two white elementary schools (Moyock and Griggs), a consolidated white high school (Knapp) and one combined elementary and high school for black students (Central). After graduating from Moyock, I expected to be a member of the freshman class of Knapp High School along with all my Moyock classmates and the graduates of Griggs, but the summer of 1965 played havoc with those expectations.

As July rolled over into August, my mother grew more anxious, my father more grim. A Board of Education member visited our house to explain personally the bottom line: public schools would be integrated by fall. In response a number of parents founded an all-white private academy. Both Mr. and Mrs. Hooper accepted positions on its staff.

What one is grateful for later doesn't always appear to be a blessing when it occurs. Discussion exhausted, the alternatives weighed and discarded, my parents sat me down to say I couldn't attend classes in the prefab aluminum building being erected in the cornfield. I had to go to Knapp. The decision upset me because most of my friends by then were going elsewhere, and if they went elsewhere I wanted to follow. My one consolation centered on Linda attending Knapp too. Neither of our families had the capital for private instruction. Unequivocally opposed to integration, our parents wished they had the money, but they didn't. There was nothing left to do or say.

For several years the county continued to operate the wholly black school. High school students enrolled there were given a "choice" of which to attend—Central or Knapp, another ploy by which the Board of Education attempted to skirt the strict letter of the law. If no black *chose* to switch, no school board could *force* a transfer, now could it?

On the grounds of Knapp High School, opening day of the term, 1965, we stood in two distinctly segregated clusters: the blacks who made the move from Central on one side of the cafeteria steps; the whites who remained at Knapp on the other. I remember it as a fog-laced morning but that could have been a reflection of my mind state, not the actual atmosphere. All of us carried the same virgin notebooks, the same Bic pens, but each side viewed the other warily, previously warned and admonished by the generation back home.

If you have to sit next to one, don't talk to him.

You've got a right to be there same as any white, no matter what she says.

Try to stand it for a year. Maybe next September we'll have the money to send you to private school.

If your friends don't transfer this year, they will next year. It's a better school, a better chance.

The ignorance that fueled our school yard standoff was sad

and sickening but, as a force of the time, inescapably real. The blacks there had been labeled troublemakers and upstarts; the whites, trash and "nigger lovers." In a sense, we were outsiders all. The fight for and against civil rights may have been our parents' version of the Civil War, but we, their children, primarily longed for the chance to enjoy high school.

And we did, given the chance. When word leaked out through the kid network that the happenings at Knapp were standard stuff—no violent confrontations in the classrooms, hallways, parking lots or elsewhere, just conference sports, study halls, tricky algebra tests, the love-giddy and the lovelorn—several who had enrolled at the new academy trickled back and joined our mottled crowd, Roseanne among them. Her two brothers, however, stayed on at the academy, as did the Hoopers.

The latter had become choosy about whom they spoke to on the street, I heard, but since I saw neither of them during my high school years, I could believe, without correction, that both would have greeted me warmly. Surrounded by neighbors who no longer spoke to each other, the bitterness of their feuds lasting long after the era of segregation had passed, I lived with evidence to the contrary. Still, I held to my assumption about the Hoopers, and for a while no person or incident proved me wrong.

At sixteen, Roseanne got pregnant. The fact wouldn't seem to connect with racial tensions but did. Within a polarized white community, her "predicament" became just another excuse to draw the battle lines and divide up sides: for or against, friend or foe.

We had grown up together, Roseanne and I, and we were flung together in all matters relating to school and play. As preschoolers, dressed identically, we sang "Sugar in the Morning" at community functions. Our mothers belonged to the Woman's Club, our fathers to the Ruritan Club. My dad bought the lime for his fields from her dad.

As a kid Roseanne was jovial and good-natured. Left alone, she probably would have been content with middle-of-the-road achievement, but her mother, Donna Marie, wouldn't stand for the mediocrity. She wanted Roseanne to look the best, sing the best, dance the best, win every contest and every award—dreams Roseanne tried to fulfill.

Sometimes when I visited her house, apropos of nothing, Donna Marie snatched her away for a whispered confab. When Roseanne returned, we picked up where we'd left off—with dolls, dice, whatever—but she'd been interrogated and around the edges the cross-examination showed. Occasionally Donna Marie demanded an on-the-spot piano and voice recital. I wasn't invited to join; my role was spectator. As I sat at the kitchen counter, jammed next to the upright piano, Roseanne pounded out "How Great Thou Art" and "You'll Never Walk Alone." She sang as loudly as she played (both styles endorsed by her mother). As I watched, Donna Marie watched me. I never figured out the best method of escaping that scrutiny—should I appear pleased? sad? jealous?—but I felt beholden to sit at attention throughout the performance and to sit quietly.

Roseanne did well in school. Naturally bright like Linda, she seldom studied. The first of our group to date, she went to the high school prom at age thirteen. The precocity that stunned our mothers wowed Roseanne's friends. He wasn't the cutest, her date, but he *drove a car.*

Even before the onset of adolescence, Roseanne liked boys without being terribly picky whom she liked and whom she let "like" her. Given the elaborate checks and balances of her mother's love, the simplicity of supply and demand must have seemed appealing. High school guys wanted girls who put out. Plus, Roseanne had other attributes: a good figure, sizable breasts. She was popular, a cheerleader. Life barreled along until one morning a drunk driver ignored the bus's stop sign and ran over her youngest brother, killing him instantly.

The community rallied around the family. Or tried. In her grief Donna Marie avoided almost everyone, including her surviving children. Roseanne stayed several nights at my house. She seemed okay, talked about her boyfriend of the time and homework. I took my behavioral cues from her. She didn't cry, didn't invite comforting. Maybe she wanted to avoid competing with her mother who was demanding the lion's share of comfort and getting it.

At the funeral Donna Marie dragged at the casket and wailed in a exhibition of public mourning new to Shawboro, but afterward the family closed in upon itself, seeing few outsiders other than the Hoopers. A month or more passed before Roseanne started sleeping through class, then cupping her mouth and running for the toilet. Even so, she kept up her grades. In May of that year we both served as graduation marshals, wearing white according to custom. As she led the seniors to their folding chairs, Roseanne's white stomach led her.

In the wake of pregnancy and death, Mrs. Hooper and Donna Marie grew very close. The remaining son continued to go to the academy, and although the father of Roseanne's baby wasn't black, there was a suggestion in the air that her "moral corruption" stemmed from association with an educational system that commingled the races. Mrs. Hooper continued to counsel the family even after Roseanne married; care that, on its surface, followed the principles of Christianity, providing solace in times of distress. Its consequence, however, seemed less positive. With the notable exception of Roseanne, the Dales settled into a pattern of expecting the worst and resenting any family who sidestepped catastrophe. As their paranoia calcified, so did their sympathies. Perhaps from years of practice, Roseanne remained her same affable self.

I was glad to escape to college, delighted to put sing-a-longs, spelling bees, the threat of teenage pregnancy, the almost incestuous physical, social and intellectual competitions of small-town life behind me. One student in a sea of 22,000, I found great relief in the anonymity and wasn't ready to give it up at Christmas break. I did because my parents expected the concession. After the days of gifts and turkey had passed, to fill a few of the empty hours, I went to a friend's basketball game—the first time I'd ventured inside the academy's gym.

Near the end of the first quarter, Mrs. Hooper arrived and sat on one of the bleachers below me. I hadn't seen her since elementary school and scrambled down, wanting to share college and my latest book list with the person largely responsible for turning a forest child into a reader. She didn't turn around when I took the seat beside her. When I tapped her shoulder, she nodded perfunctorily, then began to cheer in a style as raw as any around.

Confused and ill at ease, I joined in, thinking the cheering would unite us, but it didn't unite us. I tried asking about Mr. Hooper and her children. She answered shortly and kept her back turned squarely against me. Although I still considered myself her grateful student, clearly her attitude toward me had changed. I was being "cut," deliberately and methodically; further denial was useless and absurd. Whatever sentimental attachment I felt, to her I represented the opposition—no more, no less.

I sat there a few moments more in a kind of dazed shock,

deeply hurt but lucky, really, to be feeling the sting and helplessness of judgment by affiliation as late as eighteen. In Currituck County my black classmates had been subjected to a far harsher version of that indictment at a far more vulnerable age.

Still, I didn't feel lucky; I felt erased. Young or older, you only have to experience facelessness once to lose a certain spontaneity of trust. Afterwards you screen your candidates for idol more closely, hedge your bets, go stingy on the admiration. People, for better or worse, are required to prove themselves over a longer haul.

The long haul of that winter night in an all-white gymnasium taught me I had ceased to be one of Mrs. Hooper's favorites, and she one of mine.

Sports:
Family Style

My brother, eight years older, had his own regulation-height hoop tacked to a pine tree; I had another, half the height, tacked to the tree beside it. A good brother, Craig let me shoot hoops alongside him even at the runty stage when I lobbed the basketball from between my knees.

As a family we often played HORSE, each missed shot counting as a letter. My mother, a high school star with the photo album to prove it, made a specialty of the two-handed chest heave. With no one in front of her defending the basket, she got quite a momentum going until we got her giggling. Then her style went all to pieces. My father played with his cap on and never worked up a sweat. He took impossible shots from beyond the official playing court. Sometimes he climbed on top of the picnic table and threw over the clothes line and our heads. He kept shooting from those outer reaches, shooting and grinning, exasperating my mother, until the arc of the ball lined up perfectly with the nylon net and "swished." Still, it was my brother who won nine of ten matches. Dubby was wedded to trick shots, my mother rattled easily, and my basket percentage was poor at best. Craig relied on non-flashy jump shots from either side of the dirt court or free throws from a foul line he dug with his heel.

We recreated as a family, nuclear and extended. Every Sunday of every season the Meads clan gathered at Dora's, and once conversation lagged, we moseyed outside for games of croquet, badminton, horse shoes, softball, hardball, basketball and tennis on a root-gnarled court beneath the sycamore tree. Player age ranged from five to fifty-five; everyone participated except Dora, who oversaw events with a kind of put-upon smirk, as if she were babysitting two generations of rambunctious, yappy children.

"Look, Ma. Home run," Aunt Madeline might say as the ball headed for swamp muck.

And then perhaps Dora would reply: "About time."

My father's prime sport was baseball. A left-handed pitcher, he'd been good enough in high school to win a baseball scholarship to Wake Forest College. People said he'd had a chance at the minor leagues, but if that were an aspiration, the war ended it. With his brothers scattered in Europe, Dubby was the son who came home to farm. He didn't complain. War was war; family obligations, family obligations. And if you carried a drop of Meads blood in you, the obligation on Sunday afternoon was to play hard, play fair and never, never whine.

When I whined, blaming the size of the bat (too heavy), the color of the croquet mallet (too green), Dubby said: "Get out there and play and quit fussin'." If my brother ever whined, he stopped before I came along. I stopped before I graduated to the regulation-size hoop. You miss a shot, try again. You fall down, get up. Hurt yourself? Throw a Band-Aid on the wound and keep going.

It wasn't a terrible code to play or live by, but sometimes it was a tough one to keep.

During my mother's heyday, gymnasiums were the luxury rather than the rule. She and her high school teammates played the bulk of their games on cement slabs outdoors. Deeply offended by "glory grabbers," she had a stash of cautionary tales about swell heads who hogged the ball and lost the game. Play team, not individual, she drilled into my brother and me. Take the shot if you have it, but don't run over the rest of the pack attempting to shine.

Even without hogging the ball, my brother shone. For six years he held the high school record for points scored in a single game (twenty-eight), that glory achieved the same season his team won the tournament trophy. For tournament games, our conference, composed of small county high schools, played in the city gymnasium, an awesome place. The backboards there were fiberglass, not wood; the court was blond, not brown; smooth, not pitted; the bleachers rose to the ceiling. County fans usually cheered from a couple of rough benches designated "Home" and "Visitor."

To win anywhere was thrilling, but to win in that swank arena was the pinnacle of success. Victory night for my brother's team, as the tournament officials arranged the trophies and Craig and his flushed buddies lined up to receive their due as champions, I couldn't restrain myself. I made a beeline across the court. He was seventeen; I was nine. It was his big moment; I was his goofy kid sister. But when I grabbed his waist and squeezed, mortified or not, he didn't flinch or turn away. He hugged me back.

My basketball career officially began in seventh grade. First game out, I scored the team's first basket. After that, the opposing coach sicced his finest guard on me, and in four quarters I never got off another shot. Still, we won. We almost always won in those days, and we entered high school expecting the trend to continue. Currituck County had a reputation for excellent basketball teams, male and female.

As a high school freshman, I got to play with my cousin Linda, my pal Sharon and the legendary Alice Gregory who'd been a starter on three championship teams. At that stage of women's basketball, only two on the team could cross the center line and play both offense and defense. Smart coaches chose the fastest two, and one of them was Linda. Slower and bigger, I played stationary forward; as such, my prime contribution was supposed to be points. After Alice shook hands with the opposing captain, the game buzzer buzzed, and we took to the court, I was also responsible for the opening tip-off (Linda was too short). But if I gained control of the tap, I always batted the ball in my cousin's direction. With little or no head start, she could usually outdistance the pack for an uncontested lay-up.

We started losing early in the season, despite the stellar Alice. Once Alice graduated, we lost more frequently, and whenever we lost, I cried. To my recollection, Linda never did. Against the Creswell Wildcats, Linda scored three of the first four field goals and wasn't at all happy. I was supposed to be the shooter; why wasn't I *shooting*? Her bangs had already sweated into pitchforks; my face had already gone splotchy. We had expected to win against Creswell, a team ranked even lower than us in the conference standings, and their competitiveness surprised us.

"*Quit holding back!*" Linda screamed at me at the onset of the third quarter, after which I did begin to shoot more. Still, we lost. At the final buzzer, when no amount of effort could undo the defeat, my crying erupted mid-court. We must have been quite the sight: the little squirt of a girl comforting the lummox.

"Numskull," she hissed. "You think you lost it all by yourself?" I felt fairly sure I had, but I appreciated the contradiction. Since it came from Linda, I almost accepted it as truth.

Although we practiced hard, ran our laps, charged the goal, dove for loose balls, shot foul shots and executed passing drills, instead of victories, we racked up an even more stunning string of defeats. The fans soon deserted us, trickling in for the boys' match only. The game Craig saw, his sister couldn't hit the side of a barn. A yearbook photograph preserves my father's disappointment. Among a conglomeration of other fathers, Dubby sits, chin in hand, solemnly watching his girl child commit a grievous foul, my elbow lodged in a guard's neck.

Whenever an elbow knocked out one of Sharon's contacts, the referees stopped the game and both sides dropped to the floor to search for the lens. We usually found it—a green dot among hightops—and after licking it a couple of times, Sharon popped it back in her eye and the game resumed. But as our losing streak continued, she considered playing blind to see if a vision swag would help. We were all feeling desperate by then and very, very frustrated. Even my glory moment against Columbia brought no lasting joy. Seconds left, the ball in my hand and no time to get it to anyone else, Linda again screamed "shoot" and I did, using Mom's two-handed technique. The ball cannon-balled toward the basket, slammed hard against the backboard and by sheer luck bounced in. We were euphoric! Tied score! We could still win in overtime!

Could have, but didn't. That game we lost by a single, tear-jerking point.

After Linda graduated, the year Sharon and I became seniors, a new coach, female this time, took over the disastrous girls' team. Traditionally, co-captains got to choose their uniforms first; a small privilege, but coveted. The new coach called one, then two, then several players into the locker room before Sharon and me. By the time we were summoned, only the dregs were left. It could have been an oversight, and for a while we tried to believe it was. But the slights just kept multiplying. Team meetings convened without us; Monday mornings we heard about scrimmage sessions held the Saturday before. As the season wore on, with victories still few and far between, Sharon and I became known as "the lead butts"—a joke and not a joke. During a late-season pep rally, our coach announced to the school at large how much she looked forward to "next season" when her team could get down to "playing ball" after the "big shots" had graduated.

No one expected her to like losing—God knows, we didn't— but neither did Sharon and I expect to take full blame for the disappointment. Linda wrote "buck up" letters from college, urging me, in the spirit of family tradition, to ignore the jabs, play hard. My parents stoically sat through loss after loss. At home, after practice every day, I shot lay-ups by porch light until bedtime. If you shoot lay-ups on a goal tacked to a pine tree, you learn to feint and swerve.

For the final road game of that miserable year, we travelled to Hatteras. Hatteras had a strong team, offensively and defensively, led by the Dillon sisters who played to win but expected at least the appearance of a good fight. Sharon sat out the game because of a sprained ankle. By the end of the first quarter she must have been grateful for the injury; it spared her a whole new level of humiliation. I scored eight points, set up two other shots, even grabbed a rebound and got benched without explanation after three minutes of play.

As the second quarter moved into the third, the Dillon sisters mimed "What Gives?" in my direction. Winning by a landslide, they had time to inquire. I was glad Dubby wasn't there; I wished my mother had stayed home too. I would have preferred an entire gymnasium of strangers to one half-filled with everyone I knew. Five seconds showing on the game clock, our coach called a time out and sent me back in. I remember Sharon's curse, the outrage that broke through my mother's public mask, the too bright lights, my billion-pound resistant body. I remember our scorekeeper looking up from the check-in desk with a kind of startled, wondering pity that helped me to understand I inhabited one of those pivotal moments wherein I could act by the "code" or listen to my gut. My gut wanted blood, of course, but I wasn't my parents' child for nothing. I took my place on the court, "played" those remaining five seconds. I kept my mouth shut, head up. No whining aloud/allowed.

Obviously our team carried home no trophies at tournament time. Even if I'd had a kid sister to rush across the court, I wasn't part of any victory to inspire the trip. I did win a couple of personal citations for conference and tournament play, voted on by other coaches and players. So, in a way, by sticking out the season and refusing to quit, I won a modicum of revenge. But winning those two gold-plated miniature basketballs felt a lot like sacrificing the war for the battle. All that persevering left a permanent smear on the pastime. I no longer associated competitive sports with fun. Basketball, in particular, I associated with the stringent test: "Who Will Buckle First?"

One day many years later, while Linda and I chatted on the porch, Dubby and two of her sons played HORSE on the old backyard goal. At nine, Linda's oldest was a quiet fellow: a little clumsy, eager to please. His younger brother was the opposite: a frenetic sassy pants. For a time the game proceeded along the usual lines—shouts, dribbles, a vibrating backboard. Then the tone changed. The sassy pants started in with excuses: unfair, foul, he tripped me, I'm taking that shot over.

"Get back over here and play and quit your fussin'," Dubby advised.

But that go-around he wasn't talking to a son or even a grand-son, and his opinion carried less weight. It was left to Linda to reform the behavior of the quitter who kicked his way past us. Doing so, she seemed more my father's daughter than I did. Barely turning her head, she drawled:

"Go on then. Good riddance to you."

I watched the spoilsport glance back again and again, turning full around at his great-grandmother Dora's birdbath, waiting for and wanting someone to call him back. No one did. Dubby and the whiner's brother had returned to playing HORSE, his mother to her conversation with me. He had gone against the family code, and when he did, because he did, the family said: go, go on, good riddance.

Ras's
Place

An old postcard of The Nags Head Casino plugs it as "the largest ballroom in the South" and lists some of the famous who played there: Sammy Kaye, Louis Armstrong, Fats Domino. All very curious. It's not that I doubt owner and manager G. T. "Ras" Westcott was sharp enough to copy lie or hire a copy liar: someone who thought ballroom sounded classier than dance hall, a Sammy Kaye fan who liked to embellish, to dream a little dream. Ras was renowned for his shrewdness in business and other quasi-legal pursuits. It's just a bit of a strain matching that ballroom and musical greats description with the rough and tumble beach club patronized by my parents, my brother and myself. The Casino we knew wasn't a glittery upscale hot spot gone to seed; it was seedy at its core. Seediness contributed a major part of its attraction for 40 years.

Beginning in my parents' era, people went to The Casino to have a good time and sometimes, in the throes of that good time, people got touchy; people got their hackles up; and then people tried to beat the piss out of one another. Occasionally fights broke out on the dance floor, but mostly fights broke out at the bar. Massive quantities of drink inspired other feats of daring as well, including leaping through the huge, screenless second floor windows to the dirt parking lot below. It became a kind of sport, dirt diving, very popular among the loose and limber.

The first Saturday night my brother, in high school, made the forty-mile trip to The Casino, he broke curfew. When he did slink in several hours past midnight, my sleepless mother met him at the door. He'd had one beer, maybe several, and he paid for it. Oh how he paid. The next morning he had to leap out of bed and choke down an enormous breakfast of pancakes, eggs and bacon. Face puffy and eyes barely open, he did his best to appear chipper and ravenous, but he looked distinctly queasy. Still miffed, my mother banged and clanged the frying pan at every opportunity. All that unnecessary noise gave me a headache, and I was eight hours rested and alcohol free. Either my father had a subsequent talk with my mother or the very tradition of The Casino wore her down. Soon enough, Craig counted as a Casino regular. As long as he made it home before 1 A.M., he was allowed to sleep in—or to try while I manufactured all sorts of ungodly noise outside his bedroom door.

By the time I reached high school, my parents and their contemporaries were working overtime to convince themselves The Casino wasn't all that rowdy of a place. It had been years since the papers reported anyone sustaining serious injury from a window leap or a bouncer's fist. Fewer drunks, fewer fights, fewer broken limbs—evidence of a more subdued, civilized establishment surely. That whitewash campaign dovetailed nicely with the demographics. Their second-borns were largely female. A son at The Casino was one thing; a daughter something else entirely.

And we daughters were wild to go. Barely teenagers, we stood mesmerized in the newly paved parking lot, gazing up toward that second floor as if toward a shrine. Situated between the old beach road that paralleled the ocean and the newer bypass, The Casino was a squat, massive two-story building, shuttered in bright orange. A string of yellow lights decorated the entrance and during a sea breeze those lights knocked against each other and melodiously tinkled. The size of the building and the huge sand dunes of Jockey's Ridge behind it only reinforced its nonpareil image. Nothing on the beach came close to matching its allure or implicit promise of naughty danger. My friends and I calculated birthdays in terms of how many more would have to pass before we got to strut up those gray, paint-flecked stairs to the second floor, terrain of the in-the-know/in-the-glow Casino crowd.

Before starting grammar school, I already knew the ins and outs of The Casino's ground floor—all ages had access to it. As a family, we patronized the soda fountain and bowling alley. The soda fountain featured lots of neon, an oversized Wise Potato Chip owl, and a menu confined to burgers, shakes, fries, banana splits and ice cream sundaes. Fortified by that chow, we bowled a few games on the warped lanes in the rear. Duck pin bowling. Each turn we had three balls to knock down the pins. Given the slants and buckles of The Casino's lanes, toppling a single pin posed a major challenge. Even Dubby, a curve-ball whiz, had trouble navigating the mounds and gullies. After each turn, we had to wait for the reset. Nothing was automated, and Ras paid only one pair of busy hands to realign pins and return balls for all ten lanes. Bowling counted as a sideshow. Family stuff, little profit. The real profit, the real money, was generated upstairs.

To go upstairs, you were supposed to be eighteen. But as my underage friends and I observed from the soda fountain's red swivel stools, sucking on shakes and staring enviously at the stair crowd, lots who scaled those heights weren't anywhere near eighteen.

Precisely the kind of observation to turn one bold.

As a teenager, I stayed at the beach not only with my family, but with my friends' families. My sixteenth summer I stayed a week with Sharon and her sister's brood in a cottage at Nags Head. In exchange for nominal babysitting, we got a room to ourselves and the chance to sneak off to The Casino without our mothers being the wiser. Too pumped to wait for the weekend, we ventured there on a weeknight when those long-coveted stairs weren't the least bit jammed. Sharon and her date and I and mine got past the "No Long Hair" sign at the landing without incident, then to the cashier's booth without being pulled aside and asked for ID. We didn't look twelve, but we certainly didn't look eighteen. Regardless, the cashier collected our money, stamped us with a number only the black light illuminated and waved us along.

Legitimately "in," we might have exhaled if we hadn't been so thunderstruck. After years of imagining, we had finally entered the land of legend, hazy with cigarette smoke. The polished wood dance floor ran the length of the building, from the elevated stage on one end to the beer bar at the other. Determined daredevils could still manage a window dive, but first they had to clear the booths shoved against the windows and walls. An aisle snaked between the booths and tables that edged the dance floor. Anyone uninterested in dancing could meander indefinitely around that track, checking out who was with whom and for how long.

Sharon and I and our dates took an empty booth. No one materialized to take our drink orders. If you wanted anything to drink at The Casino, you made the trip to the bar yourself. Since a beer would have constituted sensory overload that introductory night, we passed on the alcohol and just danced. In later years, "just dancing" was totally unacceptable. Every twist and turn had to be practiced and perfected in advance. Never mind that those elaborate routines required much more space than any couple could lay claim to come the weekend. Cramped or not, the execution had to be flawless. Anything less tagged you an amateur.

Dancers at The Casino always danced to the music of black bands: The Tams ("I've Been Hurt"), The Showmen ("39-21-40 Shape") and lesser lights. The members of those bands and all the others Ras booked must have grown tired of looking out and seeing nothing but a sea of tanned white. Regardless, for as long as the Casino existed, black performed, white danced and never the twain did meet.

To keep out black customers and long-haired white customers and, theoretically, to break up fights rather than cause them, Ras hired bouncers. His bouncer specifications must have been very precise. To the man, his employees were mammoth, elaborately muscled and intricately tattooed fans of the crewcut. That choice of hairdo did nothing to disguise old "war" wounds. In certain lights, their skulls looked as if they'd been shaped by a hammer and chisel. But the battered vision effectively served as deterrent—perhaps the point all along. No Casino patron doubted that Ras's boys knew how to fight, fight hard, and win. And no one wise to those scars could reasonably conclude they'd come out of a rumble looking the same as they went in.

Still there's always someone who recklessly ignores the odds, hampered by stupidity or goaded by vanity. One of those delusional hotheads chanced on Ras's turf the summer after Sharon and I graduated high school. Full-time beachettes by then, we shared a boarding house room, flipped burgers by day at The Trading Post and partied by night, proud owners of $35, seven-nights-a-week, all-summer Casino passes, worth every penny.

The night of the brawl, Ras was doing great business—elbow to elbow people, the beer flowing nicely and closing time still hours away. To ensure the beer buying continued, bouncers circled with trash barrels, clearing the tables of empties. Or cans they declared empty. It was irksome. You bought a beer, you took a sip, you got up to dance and it disappeared. Irksome but worth going a round with a bouncer? Un-unh.

The customer who felt differently hailed from Staunton, Virginia—a "foreigner." New to The Casino and its rules, implicit and explicit, he took issue with the practice of dumping perfectly good beer. Quick to notice the *contretemps*, my date gestured toward the Virginian's twisted, yapping mouth, doing its yapping way too close to a bouncer's face. The crowd surrounding them had already fanned out, the way a crowd does, sensing trouble and making adequate room for its development without relinquishing the best views. Ras's hired hand showed more restraint than any of us expected, going so far as to turn his back on the complainer in favor of the next stash of cans.

First mistake: the Virginian charged after him.

Second mistake: he punched one of those well-muscled, intricately tattooed shoulders, and he punched it hard.

The punch was all the excuse Ras's boy needed to upend the Virginian and drag him toward the stairs. The band instinctively loudened to drown out the chaos, but by then no one paid the slightest attention to the band. Even the elusive and reclusive Ras emerged from a back room to see what all the fuss was about. In that fleeting appearance, he looked every bit as tough as his employees but his own crewcut leveled off somewhere near their armpits. Someone taller must have informed him his boys had the situation under control because he didn't linger; he left the outcome in their more than capable hands.

I didn't actually see the Virginian sail down the stairs but those closer to the action swore he did. He must have gotten some of that relaxing beer down his gullet and into his system because when he landed he broke no bones and left on his own two feet. All things considered, we blood sport spectators concluded the

ejected was a lucky bastard, but his father, a military man, thought
otherwise. Misunderstanding parochial loyalties and the incred-
ible amount of tax revenue generated by The Casino, he sued. A
waste of effort, that law suit. The local judge dismissed the case,
agreeing with Ras's definition: The Casino was an "enter at your
own risk" kind of joint. Maybe Ras and his boys celebrated their
victory in the judge's chambers or maybe, for decorum's sake, they
waited to celebrate on the paint-flecked stairs.

For all their mobsterish drama, bouncer fights were the exception, couple fights the rule at The Casino. The combination of
beer, leering rivals and dirty dancing guaranteed at least one blow-
up a night. High school sweethearts from five counties shimmied
thigh to thigh, sweat pouring. Inevitably someone rubbed up
against someone else accidentally or on purpose, rubbing a third
someone the wrong way. Accusations were leveled, excuses provided or tantalizingly withheld. Girls hissed or got teary; boys bellowed or sulked. That hideous clunky symbol of affection, the high
school ring, got flung, wax filler and all, out the window, down
the stairs, into the john. Friends tried to intervene or stayed clear.
And after the row, everybody recovered with another beer.

After the last song was sung and the last beer consumed, we
stumbled down the stairs, piled into our cars and wove our way
home, thoughtlessly confident of our ability to drink, drive and
survive. Until college, I wasn't much of a tippler, but the boyfriend
I choreographed the elaborate dance routines with thought nothing of finishing off a dozen beers by closing, and he drank fast—
no bouncer snatched his brew. Girlfriend fashion, at the end of
the night, I never grabbed the keys. Whatever his state, he always
drove home. We wore no seat belts; his Mustang had none. Young,
stupid and lucky, we went our merry way.

Back then, cops friendly with Ras winked at the sin of driving
under the influence, but a few officers did linger in the vicinity of

The Casino near closing to intercept any revelers who tore out of the parking lot and accelerated to sixty, driving in the left lane. The night my boyfriend and I got caught, we weren't travelling at any great speed, we just weren't travelling in a straight line. The officer who blue lighted us couldn't have been more polite, and true to form he wrote no ticket. He checked my boyfriend's bleary eyes and driver's license with a flashlight, leaned farther into the car and put a question to me:

"You been drinking too?"

Wildly offended by that vicious slur on the character of his Southern belle, my boyfriend brashly lied: "She's never touched a drop!"

Unimpressed with the chivalry, the officer ignored him and focused, rather wearily, on me.

"So can you drive?"

"If I wear his glasses," I qualified.

"Then wear them," he said. "They're not doing him much good."

I was a certified Casino addict in high school and in college, but as a college gal I had to make do with fewer fixes. When the desperation became too intense, friends and I made the three-and-a-half-hour trip home on spring and fall weekends, then drove another hour to the beach on Saturday night. By then a younger crowd had already replaced our group as core contingent. The power shift wasn't the reason we stopped patronizing the place, however; we stopped because The Casino ceased to be. In perhaps Ras's shrewdest business move, he sold the land and building a few months before the roof collapsed on the famous second floor. When the dust settled, those gray, paint-flecked stairs led only to open sky.

For a short time thereafter, the decapitated building housed pinball machines, but eventually the lot itself proved more valuable than the arcade business. What remained of the original structure was sold again and bulldozed. Now the property is covered with a row of cottages indistinguishable from the cottages jammed on either side. Without the marker of Jockey's Ridge, no one today would be able to locate where The Casino was when it was. The old postcard lists no milepost number and no address. Ras's choice, no doubt. Those in-the-know knew, and as for the rest, who cared?

Joe,
Leo
and Lillian

My high school stood a short walk from the county court-house, a convenience the year Joseph Linton Hurdle was tried for the murder of Leo Tulley Banks. The proximity allowed our sociology class to troop over *en masse* and observe, firsthand, the internecine workings of the judicial process. A travelling judge presided. As a district, Currituck lacked the necessary trade to occupy a Superior Court justice full time.

The inflated audience for the murder trial and the notoriety those numbers implied might have gratified another defendant. Neither seemed to faze Joe Hurdle. On the witness stand he gave the confused, barely audible responses of a man lost in a fog of vacancy. He seemed addled, scarcely aware of the people and procedures that would jail or free him. Moreover, the confusion didn't appear to be a recent development. On the contrary. Joe and befuddlement looked very much like long-term chums.

As our group strained forward to hear his testimony, he slumped, head dipping toward his chest, except on those rare occasions when his focus wandered from the floor to the blank wall at his side. He wore a shapeless suit, unfashionable even by Currituck standards. It was also a shabby suit, and Joe Hurdle wasn't a poor man. He owned land, lots of it. That acreage was the very asset that attracted Mrs. Lillian Sawyer, the pundits said. Without that money maker, Leo Banks's already married daughter wouldn't have given old Joe, at sixty-four, the "time of day."

My class missed Lillian's hour on the stand—a shame because that testimony, or that part she was allowed to give, counted as a highlight and the crux of further scandal. She testified in favor of Joe and against her father, the deceased, offending most of the county and all of her kin. About that alignment, the pundits said this: Lillian always did know the buttered side of her bread, and there was a more lucrative Last Will and Testament than her father's to consider.

All in all our day in court disappointed. It packed none of the white-knuckle excitement we'd expected. The judge, Joe Hurdle's vocal twin, also muttered—a more authoritarian mutter than the defendant's, but difficult to understand all the same. After much prompting, Joe gave his name and occupation (farmer), his address and a few more incidentals before appearing to fall asleep. We were equally disappointed in the lawyers, neither an orator born. Primed for a live enactment of "Perry Mason," replete with suspense, smoldering secrets and tortured, emotional unravelings, we got instead a non-event.

Where was the drama, the impact?

A memory fudge, I decided later. Surely there were all grades of drama operating in that courtroom; I just hadn't known where to look.

When I finally got around to investigating, I returned to a

courthouse virtually unchanged by 25 years and the escalating
demands of rapid population growth. The same modest brick
building, located next to the Currituck Sound and within view of
the Knotts Island ferry landing. The same slightly bowed cedar
trees, shading the entrance. Inside, the same gritty linoleum floor
tiles and slow-turning ceiling fans. And throughout every room
and corridor, the same musty smell of old papers, dutifully filed
away and forgotten.

Conveniently, the current Registrar of Deeds was the mother
of one of my 1968 classmates and cheerfully agreed to unearth
the court records of the trial both her son and I attended. But
before she undertook that search, we danced the manners dance,
accepted by both sides as a necessary (and civilized) step within
the procedural sequence. I asked about her son Kenny's current
fortunes, his wife and kids. She asked where I was living and did I
plan to stay home for a while or was this just another one of those
in and out visits?

The inquiry/revelation combo reestablished my legitimacy.
After a third sentence or so I sounded "completely normal" (i.e.,
like a native). Plus, I belonged to Ann and Dubby, respected citi-
zens who paid their taxes, attended church and to date had been
convicted of no crimes.

The Hurdle file, handed over, felt suspiciously thin—and for
good reason. The manila folder held no blow-by-blow account of
the trial, only a summation of the testimony, the verdict and a
petition for appeal.

Maybe the transcript got lost, or maybe the court stenographer took it with her when she retired, the Registrar of Deeds
suggested with remarkable indifference. She herself wasn't responsible for the missing, she reminded me, only the actual, and the
actual recorded this: Joe Hurdle was convicted of the man-

slaughter of Leo Banks and sentenced to "confinement in State Prison for a term of no less than eight or more than twelve years."

A thin file, but rich.

In 1968 Otis Stone owned a grocery store located between Sligo and Moyock, a popular lunch spot for nearby farm workers as well as the highway trade. Otis owned the lot the store was built on; Joe Hurdle owned the surrounding farmland. Mrs. Ruth Banks, Leo's wife and Lillian's mother, worked for Otis, and the October eleventh that Joe Hurdle drove up and Leo Banks was driven away dead, her daughter stopped by for a visit around noon.

If Ruth Banks testified, her statement didn't make the file. The pages quote only Joe, Lillian and one other eye witness, my wrong place/wrong time cousin Bobby Meiggs.

Joe Hurdle didn't go into Otis's store October 11. He sat in his car in the parking lot, waiting to pick up one of his field hands, according to his testimony. The fall had been a warm one, and the day was hot. For ventilation, Joe rolled down the window on the driver's side. A few minutes later Leo Banks ran from the store, "waving his arms" and shouting words Joe couldn't decipher. Then the shouter whirled around and ran back in.

Lillian Sawyer's name first appears on page four of the surviving five-page appeal document. During the trial she testified that her father "burst out of the store, cursing (and) throwing his hands up" shortly after the defendant arrived. When the defense asked: "What did he say?" the prosecution objected, and the objection was sustained. Therefore, the appeal papers argued, Lillian was prevented from repeating what she would have repeated "had she been permitted to answer." Specifically, that Leo screamed at Joe: "You common son of a bitch, get the hell off the road. I mean leave here now. You are not fit to live here or stay here."

Although Joe Hurdle testified that he understood none of the content of that outburst (strange, given the open window), his lawyers maintained that he understood the "menacing" nature of the accompanying gestures. In reaction he moved to the middle of the car seat and closer to his pistol, prepared, if necessary, to act in self-defense.

Inside the store, Leo Banks pulled a rifle from under the counter and started out again, my cousin Bobby testified. With some difficulty, Bobby and Ruth Banks successfully wrestled the gun from Leo and calmed him down. Thereafter he sat with his wife and friend, talking quietly. After he finished his lunch, he announced he had to get back to work.

Leo said he was leaving for work, not to kill Joe Hurdle, and he left the store unarmed, my cousin repeated under oath. Whatever Leo's original intentions, the sight of Joe Hurdle still there, still waiting, enraged him all over again. And this time when he approached the car, the driver picked up the pistol, aimed through the open window, fired, started the engine, engaged reverse and sped away.

In a mutter at least the stenographer must have understood, the defendant repeated Leo's last threats:

"'You son of a bitch, I'm going to drag you out of this car and kill you. . . . I know you've got a gun, but you ain't got nerve enough to use it.'"

"To keep him from killing me," Joe Hurdle swore, he pulled the trigger.

If so, the strategy worked brilliantly. Only one body gave up the ghost. The bullet entered Leo's body at the lower end of the breast bone, travelled through the large blood vessels of the stomach, continued through the liver and kidneys and eventually lodged in the lumbar vertebra, causing the victim to bleed to death internally before he received medical attention.

The legal argument for appeal was based not only on the exclusion of Lillian's full testimony—a possible breach of Joe Hurdle's right to a fair and just trial—but also on the State v. Minton precedent, in which a higher court ruled that uncommunicated threats were indeed admissible evidence in cases of homicide.

Along with the appeal petition, Joe Hurdle's counsel simultaneously filed papers to excuse him from a second trial for medical reasons. Three local physicians agreed on diagnoses of Parkinson's disease, arteriosclerosis and hypertension. One described Joe Hurdle's "shuffling gait," "unkempt appearance," "fixed facial expression" and, in some detail, the "holes burned in his shirt" from cigarette ashes.

The Registrar of Deeds confided that a sizable number of county residents believed "the crook" had bought off the courts, bought off the judge and, more audaciously still, pedaled past the courthouse the very day the appeal hearing was postponed due to his fragile health. A man given to semi-catatonic reveries and foot shuffles gleefully biking past the courthouse—it must have been quite the sight. In any case, Joe Hurdle did remain free on a ten thousand dollar bond and died without spending a single night in jail.

Lillian Sawyer's reputation didn't improve in the wake of the trial either. She came from nothing, was nothing, gossip sneered. Only a piece of trash testified against a father, even if that trashy testimony guaranteed her a "pretty penny" once old man Joe "croaked."

I would love to hear from Lillian's own lips whether the

attraction was purely financial and which of the two she misses more, now that they're both dead and gone. But I can't appear on her doorstep, babbling: *You don't know me, but I'm Ann and Dubby's girl, and when I was in high school my sociology class sat in on your father's murder trial, and although I missed your particular day in court, I was just wondering. . . .*

I have no valid access. I didn't go to school with her son and worse: I'm related to the witness who graphically described her father staggering and falling to the ground while the survivor, the man for whom she testified, fled the scene.

What
Miss Elizabeth
Told Me about Life

"September 27, 1904 is when I was born. Proud of it. Proud to be here.

"I've been a 4-H Club member long as I can remember. Started in Moyock. We were improving our rooms, learning to make them more attractive, more livable. And we were learning to cook things different in those days.

"We looked forward to going to camp every summer over to the Coast Guard Station at Nags Head. Had to carry our food with us, a week of food, because there weren't any stores nearby or even homes, then. One year we carried dressed chickens. We told the agent those chickens weren't going to keep and when we got over there, sure enough, we had twenty or thirty chickens we had to bury in a sand hill because they had spoiled. Miss Everett, she was. Miss Everett.

"I went away to college because my mother made me go. In fact my mother went with me because I was so timid then. As far as I had been away from home was up on the James River and

Norfolk. I didn't want to leave home, so she went to stay two or three days with me. I was engaged at the time. I went to prepare to be a better mother and a housekeeper. That's what my mother stressed. If I didn't go to work, I could be a better mother.

"I went to Louisburg College for two years. I was mighty homesick. At Thanksgiving I packed my suitcase to come home for Christmas. The girls at the college didn't believe it—they'd come around and look under my bed at that suitcase ready to go home.

"Then I taught school for two years. Home economics. I taught one year at Bunn about 12 miles from the college and the next year I taught at Salemburg. The reason I taught different schools, the teachers left and they wanted someone to finish out the year and I went and finished out the year.

"Then, when I got married, we went to Baltimore to live. I was in Baltimore a year because my husband was finishing medicine. And from there we went to Meyersville in Maryland, near Fredericksburg, and stayed for five years. He went there to practice medicine. It was a small place then.

"Have you ever been homesick? There's never been anything any worse."

"I came back to Currituck in '35, during the Depression, to live with my family. I was divorced then. I had a child died with appendicitis at three and a half years old. My husband and I were divorced about six months later.

"Virginia Edwards, the home agent, came up to the house and said if I wanted some work to be to the courthouse Monday morning, that everyone was going down there to register for work with the WPA. And of course I was bright and early down there and got a job working as a filing clerk. Then a new program was developed, Farmers Home Administration, and I went to work for that.

"I was the home supervisor and Tully Williams was the farm supervisor. We saw the farm families who applied for loans in Currituck, Camden, Perquimans, Chowan, seven counties in all. There was a committee in each county set up of men. Didn't use women then, they were all men, and that committee approved or turned down the loans. Tully made the farm plan—how much it took to operate the farm with. Then I had to make the home plan—how much it took to live on, financially. I taught them, if they didn't know how to, to can food and live at home. We always got them garden seed and a pressure cooker. Another thing was a milk cow. Over in Murfreesboro one man didn't want a milk cow. His wife was dead, and he had to milk it, so he always called me 'Miss Cow Tail' when I went up there. He was upset over that. 'Miss Cow Tail,' he called me.

"With a milk cow you could make American cheese. We used an old oyster can and thick piece of wood with holes bored in it. Then you let that milk turn to cottage cheese and put butter coloring in there, cheese coloring, and mold it. During the Depression you couldn't buy cheese. If you were going to have it, you had to make it. We canned sweet potatoes too. One woman in Perquimans County, every time she saw me years after said, 'I'm still canning sweet potatoes.'

"You just went into the home and did whatever was necessary. If the clothes lines and wood piles were in the front yard, we had to get them in the backyard. You'd want them to clean up the general appearance of their home. And fix broken-down doorsteps. So many legs were broken, crippled by broken-down doorsteps. I hadn't realized that before. So we were doing safety as well as appearance.

"Then you tried to give them something to live for. I never

will forget what our state woman said one time: if you went in a house and saw flowers stuck down in a fruit jar or something, always remember there was something nice about that woman and give her plenty of attention. Because she was trying.

"A lot of people needed dental work, a lot needed glasses, some of them needed tonsils removed. We saw to that too. One man's family needed five pairs of glasses. Five pairs in that one family. We drove up one day, Tully and myself, and all five of them came out to greet us, so proud of those glasses, you know.

"It was interesting to see how things improved. I remember one family in Camden County, a black family. Their house burned. They had a large hen house and they were living in that hen house. The children were always upset and crying when we went there. But the woman was real smart, she just hadn't had the opportunity. So we got her a cow and hogs and chickens, and she got to feeding her family and preserving and canning and those children were soon back in school. And several times after then when she'd see me she'd tell me what that had meant to her. And you could tell it from the health of her family. Every family didn't do that well, but you don't expect it.

"Another family I worked with, Claude Wright's family, he had lost his wife but he kept those two children and I admired him for that. He did the best he could. But it was one of the worst houses—dirty, junky. He never hung anything up. I shouldn't tell you this, but I went there, he was in the hospital, and I took his two children and we cleaned that house up. I screwed some hooks up side the wall and we hung those clothes. I took off a truck load of old magazines and old clothes. Stuff that needed to be thrown out. I had no business doing that, but you get attached and I admired what he was trying to do. There was a hole in the floor and I covered that up to keep the cold air from coming through. And when I got home, my second husband, Sam, said, 'You shouldn't have done that. That was his bathroom.' And sure enough, when I went back he had taken that board up. It was his bathroom.

"We mostly saw six or eight families a day. If you didn't do anything but listen to their problems and their troubles, it released something. It did them good.

"Twelve years I worked with the WPA. Then they turned the women off the Farmers Home Administration, after the Depression was over. Kept one woman, that was all they kept on the payroll. I had borrowed $1,000 to buy a car one Saturday and the next week I lost my job. And I thought what in the world am I going to do to pay that money back? I was in Hertford and I called my husband and I said, 'Sam, my job's going to be over in thirty days. What am I going to do about my thousand dollars?' He said, 'Well, hush your crying and come on home.' Said, 'You've never heard of anyone starving in Currituck in your life.'"

"So I came home and I sold Fuller brushes and cosmetics and paid my thousand dollars back. Then I went to work at the Carotoke Restaurant in Shawboro. I had a cook and a dishwasher and a waitress, and I was manager. It was a nice place for the community people, a nice meeting place for them, I mean. We were open breakfast, lunch and dinner and Saturday night folks came in to dance. But it wasn't enough business to operate. Johnny Etheridge said if I could get somebody to work like me, I wouldn't have to be paying all those others, but you can't find that. If a woman's going to cook, she don't want to wash dishes.

"Years don't mean a thing to me. Seems like it was '45, but I'm not sure. No, it was '51. In '51 I went to work as the home demonstration agent for Currituck County. Extension work. I did that for 18 years. Extension started in 1903 or 1904, way before the WPA. But during the Depression people needed something else. The extension service didn't lend money. The Farmers Home Administration did. They let people stay on the farm.

"About the time I started as agent, Alma Roberts started writing for the newspaper. And she didn't know how to condense at all, so she put everything in there. We had so many write-ups about things being done in Currituck—that did club work more good than anything else.

"They're called homemaker clubs now but they were called home demonstration clubs then because the county agent would go to the meeting and give a demonstration. I had fourteen clubs throughout the county and a lot of them met at night. We'd demonstrate the different kinds of food you'd prepare or some sewing. We'd do household furnishings, refinishing furniture, upholstering furniture. When I started in '51, the state wouldn't let you do crafts. They thought it was a waste of time. But I did crafts anyway. I just didn't put them in the report at the end of the month. Now the state's paying people to go out and teach crafts. Times change. They sure do change.

"We made mats out of pine needles and braided rugs and we made Christmas decorations. Crafts have been a livelihood for a lot of women. Mattie Burgess sold her angels at the Christmas Shop in Manteo as long as she was able to make them. Her picture came out in one of the oil company's magazines. She was using their Fluffo margarine cans. We had fashion shows too. It was a good time. A good time to visit. And if you didn't learn from the agent, you learned from someone else that night. And then so many people got up to speak. Not a year or two ago they called me to give a talk to the county commissioners. I said, 'I can't do it now. Last time I tried to talk I just gave out of breath'—being nervous and my age and all. And the woman who called said, 'Will you give me some notes so I can do it?' and that night the first thing she told them when she stood up, she said, 'I'm going to talk tonight because club work has put confidence in me.' And that's what I've liked to see. Women who developed.

"I know one time I was talking to Miss Alice Scaff about going to church or going to a club meeting. I told her I'd put church first because I think you should put church first and she said, 'Let me tell you something: no, you don't. You put club first and train them how to talk in church.' That's not right, that's not the way I feel, but I think club work does train leaders for your community. You still have a lot of women out there who are timid because they have never worked outside the home. They're afraid to express themselves; they think they may be wrong. And every person is a special person, each person, I don't care who they are or anything about them, each person has something to give and if you pull it out of them or help them find it, then they develop. Seeing a timid woman getting up and being able to express herself is one of the nicest things I know of.

"I've been retired since '69, but a lot of people still call me with their personal problems. If you just listen, it'll help them. Just last week I started to leave a woman's house and she said, 'Sit down.' Said, 'I've got to ask you something. One daughter-in-law wants me to live at her house and the other one wants me to stay here.' Said, 'What am I going to do?' Said, 'Please tell me what to do.' I said, 'You're old enough to do what you want to do. You and I have gotten to that age now when we can do whatever we want to do.'

"People sometimes just want you to tell them what to do but you don't. Help them see the choices, but leave it up to them. Then they can't come back and say, 'See, you shouldn't have told me. . . .' It takes a long time to learn that, but you learn it after a while.

"I had a state man come by and interview me, wanted to know

what problems I had in the county and who had ever talked ugly to me. I said I didn't have any problems and no one ever talked ugly to me.

"Some of the other agents said, 'You always laugh at everything. You never take anything personally.' I've just always been that way. Could understand why people did things and all. I went in a house one time and this young boy said, 'Mama, everything brightens up when Miss Elizabeth comes in.' And I thought, well now, I've never thought about that. But I thought it was real nice, him saying so."

Native
Son

For several years, during farming's off season, my father and Pierce's father, Bert, worked together as electricians, plumbers and general handymen around the community. Both Dubby and Bert were small-time farmers, renting what land they farmed— Dubby from his mother, Bert from whomever he could persuade. Between them, possibly, they cultivated a total of three hundred acres. Raising a family required additional revenue.

I think of Fran—Bert's wife, Pierce's mother—as the woman she was then: a dynamo of energy, athletic, tough. She helped Bert in the fields and always volunteered to drive as many of the team as could fit in her car to basketball or baseball games played else-where. Several times a week she stopped by our house before eight in the morning to drink coffee with my mother. The caffeine con-sumption helped, I'm sure, but by the time I rolled out of bed, still woozy from sleep, they'd both been awake and raring to go for hours.

Our families took a vacation together to Washington, D.C.,

the year I was nine and Pierce was ten. We all panted up the steps of the Washington Monument and toured the Washington Zoo. I still have photographs of Pierce and me, wearing souvenir caps with feathers, posing alongside the seals. He photographed cute at ten and became cuter. Beyond working in the fields, he did nothing to develop or maintain his physique, but it was a remarkable physique nonetheless. Broad chest, narrow waist, muscles—before muscles became a cultural given, an expectation. When Pierce was sixteen the preacher asked him to hang from a mock cross for the Easter pageant. It wasn't a speaking role; it was a body role. Pierce simply hung there—a mute, bare-chested, crucified Jesus, wearing gym shorts instead of a loin cloth.

In Currituck County the cute didn't really need a brain. Our student population was so tiny, everyone belonged to every club. Parents shared the family cars. We started dating young—switching off partners, switching back. As a high school sophomore, I'd already called Pierce my boyfriend a dozen times.

During his senior year, Pierce primarily dated Michelle, a cheerleader. Unlike the rest of the squad, Michelle was neither petite nor especially peppy. She'd made the cut because of a strong, low-pitched, froggy voice, audible from one end of the gym to the other.

In the locker room before the start of an afternoon's basketball and cheerleading practice, someone made the mistake of repeating aloud what everyone already took for granted: that Pierce would screw anything that moved. In the adjoining bathroom, Michelle was changing into shorts and tennis shoes. At first no one realized she had overheard. It must have taken her a few moments to work up the courage to confront us all—but she did, with her beet-red face and froggy voice, in a kind of keening speech that insisted not "everybody" who dated Pierce "did that." Victim of the female high school conundrum—screw and deny or don't screw and regret—she couldn't win.

"Sure, sure," someone else said the moment she finished because we felt, almost to the girl, sincerely sorry that she'd overheard, sorrier that the overhearing prompted a speech that convinced no one.

Common knowledge: after three weekends, Pierce demanded put out or get out, and Michelle and Pierce had been going steady (at least on her side) for almost four months.

A year out of high school, on the recommendation of their local draft board, Pierce and Lucian—Pierce's best friend and my first cousin—were screened for service in Vietnam. As Lucian described the scene, the military personnel in charge took one look at Pierce's killer body, wanted it fighting on their side and wanted it badly. Lucian had lost a toe to a lawnmower, was fifty pounds overweight, flat-footed and short, but just to make certain no one imagined Basic Training could mold his body into comparable killer shape, for several days prior to the examination he gorged on sweets.

They were assigned separate waiting lines, and while Lucian was ridiculed for his flab and attitude, Pierce was brown-nosed. They needn't have worked so hard, Lucian said. Pierce was ripe for the plucking. He already had a brother in Vietnam; his family believed in military service; his glory days as a high school linebacker were behind him, and he didn't have the grades, the money or the inclination to pursue college athletics. How else could he test that body?

Affectionately, sadly, Lucian recalled: "The dick didn't have sense enough to be scared shitless."

Lucian saw Pierce once more between his Parris Island training and departure for Southeast Asia. They went out for a nostalgic night on the "town." But the old days, like Pierce's football career, were a bygone. Even after a string of beers, the indoctrinated Marine walked and talked like a robot, all business, not an ounce of ingenuousness left. He spoke of "getting the Cong," defending "the American Way," a staunch supporter of the "my country—love it or leave it" axiom. He even got on Lucian's case, knocking him for his deliberate "wimp-out."

"Scary," Lucian told me.

He told Pierce: "What's all this crap, man? You're talking to Lucian, your buddy. Remember?"

"And?" I asked.

"Didn't blink an eye. Gung-ho through and through."

Pierce only stayed overseas a few months. In that phase of the war, pregnant girlfriends could still bring you home, and Michelle was certifiably pregnant—doctor-examined, doctor-proved. The Salvation Army found him before he had the chance to test his prowess, truly test it, by surviving the heat, the dysentery, the jungle, the ultimate one-on-one confrontation. He was discharged for accomplishing what most males could, what millions had. Shot toward a target egg, his sperm had connected.

Back home, he again farmed with his father, began to drink heavily, to bloat the killer body, to hate the woman he blamed for stealing from him the challenge of war. He drank with a kind of lost-cause vengeance, Lucian said, settling prematurely into the looks and habits of a hopeless middle age—a difficult process to watch.

They named the baby Sarah, and Bert and Fran at least were thrilled. Economics sent Michelle back into the work force almost immediately. Crop prices continued their downward spiral; farm debts accumulated. Even before a two-family split, profits were negligible. The once inexhaustible, exuberant Fran developed rheumatoid arthritis and within a few years of its diagnosis became confined to a wheelchair. Following much miserable togetherness, Michelle and Pierce acrimoniously divorced. Michelle moved to Virginia and remarried. Pierce continued to live in their trailer, continued to drink. A younger woman fell in love with him nonetheless and moved in. She also wanted marriage and, after five years or so, Pierce reluctantly agreed.

Around that time, coming off the river with Dubby at twilight, I re-met Pierce. As a joke he pretended to be the game warden, demanding a show of our fishing licenses, an explanation as to why our boat lacked running lights. Between my myopia and the fading light, I thought he might well be the game warden and a stranger.

Then Dubby started to laugh.

"Don't you know who that is?" he asked.

"Naw, she don't know, Mr. Dubby."

The Mr. Dubby salutation gave him away. Nobody but Pierce called my father *Mr. Dubby*. To cover my initial confusion, I hugged Pierce hard. But standing next to him, side by side, on the basis of appearance alone, I never would have recognized him. He didn't faintly resemble the football star I remembered.

When the scandal broke, my mother called north with the news. Sarah had confided in a school social worker; Michelle had filed charges. Pierce sat in the county jail, waiting for Bert to scrape together his bail. For almost three years of Saturdays, after her stepmother left for shopping, Sarah climbed into bed with her father, ostensibly to watch TV.

In the history of the county, no one had been tried for incest. Fran and Bert stuck by their son, as did his second wife. His parents believed in his innocence, but whether his wife believed or merely stood by him remains an open question. She wasn't a Shawboro native. Her links were elsewhere, and she shared no confidences with her neighbors. The rest of the community divided. Most in residence had known Pierce since his birth. There were a few eager to believe "any smut shoveled" in local parlance, but many more who couldn't conceive of his being capable of such a crime. His first-grade teacher, an elderly woman by then, railed at any who cast aspersions his way, wagging her finger and correcting the misinformed. She *knew* Pierce; she had taught the boy, for heaven's sake. He would *never* do such a thing.

Her support might have been genuine, but her argument was weak. It had the thunder and logic of a black and white, first-grade universe. This is right; this is wrong. He did it; he didn't do it. The six-year-old boy, the one more interested in fighting and recess than learning and books, had become a thirty-three-year-old disillusioned man by the time of her defense. It was unlikely that any of us who had "known" him before knew him then.

The majority opinion was less an opinion than a cautious, undeclared silence. People were still trying to reconcile the image of aw-shucks Pierce, wild around the edges but unfailingly polite, a bit of a drinker but a good son to Bert and Fran, with that of a depraved child abuser. They were wondering how or why a daughter would invent such a story, pondering the likelihood that any ex-wife, no matter how vindictive, would put her child through such torture for reasons of purely personal revenge.

At the trial, lawyers for the defense tried various strategies to undermine Sarah's account. They emphasized the tendency of children to "invent things," to embroider the real with fantasy. Although no one cited Freud, much was made of little girls fixating on their daddies, of wanting to be held, cuddled, loved and adored. They lobbied hard for the supremacy of the adult version of truth. Was the court really prepared to accept a child's word over a parent's? They reviewed Pierce's accomplishments: an outstanding high school athlete, a patriot who'd been willing to risk his life for his country. And finally, with Sarah on the witness stand, they tried to invalidate her testimony by confusing her into an inconsistency.

In that capacity, they failed. As upsetting as that ordeal must have been, Sarah kept to her original account. And, in the end, it was her account the court believed.

A jury of his peers convicted Pierce, after which the judge sentenced him to a stay in Raleigh's Central Prison, a maximum security lock-up, in the spring of 1984. He spent sixty days in the company of murderers and other hard core offenders at the taxpayers' expense before the court approved Bert's hardship petition. To farm, to meet his own obligations, familial and financial, Bert needed the help of his son. He couldn't manage alone. It was true; he couldn't and, because he couldn't, the court paroled Pierce.

One of the odder requirements of that parole was his mandatory appearance at all Sunday church services and Wednesday night prayer meetings. Pierce fulfilled those obligations without fail, arriving just before the first hymn ended, leaving just before the benediction prayer, sitting on the very last row of pews just as he had as a teenager.

For a while after his release, the entire family stayed out of the public eye as much as possible, ashamed or embarrassed or both. Bert, who'd always eaten lunch at the local store with the other farmers, exchanging crop prices over ham and white bread sandwiches, ate elsewhere. Fran, house-bound, rebuffed all visitors, even those who visited the community's sick and troubled as a matter of course. Very few saw Pierce other than to glimpse his coming or going from church. If he resumed drinking, he did so in the privacy of his trailer behind drawn blinds or in his truck parked on one of his daddy's rented acres, reachable by field paths and back roads. Even Lucian gave up trying to stay in touch when it became clear Pierce preferred to be left alone.

As the days, then weeks, passed, the newness of the scandal and its immediate aftermath grew old. Gossip moved on to other quarry, as gossip will. Fresher tales and innuendoes begged to be spread, even if those latest tidbits failed to pack the punch of illicit sex and prison and a family divided. Pierce and his troubles faded from the collective memory as others took hold. Eventually Bert returned to the store for his lunches, helping the clerk pump gas as he had before the trial and conviction. Pierce began to be seen out and about: at the store with his daddy, at the grain bins, in the fields grumbling about expensive fertilizer, broken cultivators, about anything except the dangerous subjects of ex-wives and children, his fellow farmers giving him every opportunity to show himself to be no moral monster, no satanic ogre, just the "same old Pierce."

Yet entirely apart from his guilt or innocence, from the truth or lie that he repeatedly raped his daughter and swore her to silence, Pierce the undisputed drunk lived stone cold sober through an incest conviction and within a locked and guarded cell for sixty days and sixty nights. He heard his child accuse him; he saw his parents suffer; he lost the freedom to come and go at will. I seriously doubt he remained—or could remain—the same old Pierce. No human is that immune.

When I visited home in June of that year, Lucian and I took one of our annual rides around the county in his pickup, surveying the dwindling farmland, the new and sprawling pockets of development. They were the same roads we'd travelled as teenagers, and they weren't the same, not by a long shot.

I asked Lucian bluntly, because I could ask anything of him bluntly, whether he believed in Pierce's guilt.

"The hour I heard, I called," Lucian answered. "And I said to him: 'Pierce, I'm here and I'm your friend, and if I can help you, let me.' And he said: 'I can't say a word. My lawyers told me to keep my mouth shut.' And that was that. Like he was back in the military. He had his orders and he was following them and nothing I could say made any difference."

"But do you *think* he did it?" I asked.

He tried not to think about it, Lucian said, because every time he did he got mad as hell and then inconsolably sad for Bert and Fran and Michelle and of course, most particularly, for Sarah.

"You think thirteen is so young and innocent, and then you find out it's older than anyone should ever live to be."

Duties
During the
Summer of 1980

When there hasn't been any rain to speak of, as there hasn't been this spring and summer, you know a field truck is coming in advance by the dust. Clouds of the stuff rise and hover above the acres of corn that stand between us, the graders stationed grader-side, and the potato patch. Once the dust clouds spiral, you hear the distant grind of a straining, badly tuned engine, an echo that gets louder with each closer quarter mile. Finally the culprit itself appears, rounding the last curve, a gritty vision stirring up more grit.

Depending on the driver, five to ten minutes elapse between the first sighting of dust and the field truck's arrival flush against the grader. Once on the tray, the produce tumbles toward a second conveyor through which the smaller, or B grade, drop. Only the A's roll toward us, the human sorters. Our job is to make sure the "big" also qualify as the "good." Bruised and rotten spuds, dirt clods, compressed beer cans, weeds, snakes and turtles we toss before the belt narrows and dumps what remains into a tractor trailer destined for a chip factory in Indiana, Ohio or Pennsylvania.

To fill one tractor trailer requires four to four and a half field loads. During one twelve-hour period, in our best effort thus far, we sent seven rigs back into traffic. But that was a day when the field trucks were lined up and waiting on us, not a day like today when we turn again and again to search for dust and see instead only currents of undulating heat.

Five of us work the grader—two male, three female. One operates the tray, the rest of us sort. Today, in the third week of digging, in oppressively hot July, when a driver brings word from the field ("one digger's busted; the other won't work"), our standard ten-hour workday automatically lengthens. There have been delays caused by broken pulleys, defunct carburetors and flat tires, but a broken digger is serious trouble.

"Lucky to get out of this hole by midnight," someone says, and the complaint gets picked up and endlessly repeated.

Bad news for the high school kids with dates; bad news for me and my swollen ankles; bad news for the long-distance truckers, losing precious road time. Worse still for Baxter Williams, proprietor, who through his dusty office window can observe five on his payroll loafing because there's nothing else we can do.

"That's potatoes for ya," somebody says, but the philosopher isn't Baxter Williams.

Into our third week as working partners, we graders have already cross-referenced our kin, discussed every preference of dress and drama. Nothing fresh gets exchanged. We're left with gripes about scrawny potatoes, heat, dust, fatigue and the revalidation of kick-ass reputations.

("Son, you wouldn't of believed how much I drunk last night. Swear to God, son, when I woke up this morning, I didn't know where in the hell I was."

"Shit, man, I drink that much for breakfast.")

("You don't believe that Firebird'll do sixty in ten? Put your money where your mouth is, fool. I'll take it. I ain't proud.")

The gals prefer a more discreetly malicious brand of gossip. ("He'll marry her if she's pregnant. You know he will.")

Another thirty minutes come and go and still no dust or word as to when any might be expected. The long-distance truckers stretch out in or under their cabs, stockpiling sleep while they can. The rest of us gravitate to the farm office and its electric fan. There, talk revolves around the upcoming wedding. As soon as the potatoes are in, Baxter's son and eldest will marry. His bride has picked out china and crystal patterns but forewent sterling because (as she explains) "not even relatives will shell out for silver nowadays."

Her soon-to-be father-in-law winces. Yields are down fifty bags per acre from last year. To fill contracted quotas, those potatoes not forthcoming from the field will have to be purchased elsewhere at market price, and they won't come cheap.

"Potatoes!" someone yells and once again we pull on gloves caked with dirt, gulp water and converge at the base of a contraption that resembles a mechanical ostrich. Because the truck careens into the final stretch in under five minutes, we know who the driver is before we can identify his features.

Every run, Eddie Rose practices two-wheeled control of a four-wheeled vehicle.

Every morning Eddie arrives for work dressed in bib overalls and a t-shirt. By his first potato delivery, the t-shirt is off; by the second, the bib hangs. By local standards he qualifies as "a big boy," the *big* more accurate than the *boy*. At twenty he weighs in at two hundred plus. Generally he farms with his father, but because their soybeans were already planted and Baxter needed him, he's currently working here.

"Goddamn, it's hot," he says, bolting from the cab. Slue-

footed, almost obscenely good-natured, he pours the entire contents of a water thermos over his head. Then he climbs onto the
platform to help sort while his truck empties. He grades without
gloves, a cigarette dangling. If he's finished his own pack and
can't bum one, he sings Barbara Mandrell tunes with two of the
other graders. Today, amid the roar and rumble, I discover he's
cousin to Charlene, an elementary school pal since moved to
Georgia.

"You really that old?" he asks.

I'm really that old.

His next question is no shocker either. Why, at my *advanced
age*, am I grading potatoes?

"Temporarily broke," I say.

He whistles through his teeth. He's thinking, every inch of
his Cracker self proclaims it, that this is what happens to females
who have no men to support them. A crying shame, that's what it
is, a crying shame. I'm semi-hoping he'll make the mistake of
expressing that sentiment aloud. But he stops short, confines
himself to deep sighs and head shakes. Why kick a poor man-
less woman when she's down?

Thanks to Jimmy Carter (or perhaps Billy Carter), good old
boys enjoyed a brief media revival, a blitz that cemented the ster-
eotype and simultaneously rang its death knell. Overexposure will
pervert a form, no matter how entrenched. I seldom run across
the fake or the genuine article anymore, but the originals displayed (among other aggravating traits) a naiveté Southern
women never shared. They were a species who defined right and
wrong in absolute terms, men who seldom, if ever, described
themselves as confused.

If Eddie Rose had the tiniest inkling that I view him as the

representative of a dying breed and not as the wit and swashbuck-
ler he takes himself for, he'd never again behave naturally in my
presence. He'd duck his head, shuffle his feet, clam up entirely.
To get him to talk about more than weather, potatoes or his
cousin Charlene, I have to tread carefully. But Eddie Rose owes
me, and he knows it. I've admitted to being old and broke. I've
answered his questions without hedging—detrimental revelations in his opinion. Now he's honor-bound to return the favor.

What I want Eddie Rose to answer without hedging is why,
sometime between now and July 31, in compliance with the Military Selective Service Act, he'll willingly record his birth date, gen-
der, social security number, telephone number and current
mailing address, officially declaring himself a Currituck County
resident awaiting transfer when thousands of his peers are refusing to register for the draft.

"Well, there's the ten thousand dollar fine," he says, but when
he sees I'm not impressed by that comic smoke screen, he turns
instantly, deadly serious, rearranging his face in what must be an
imitation of his father's expression when all joking has been set
aside.

He'll register, he says, because it's his "duty" to register, and if
he's "called to serve," he'll serve because that's his duty also.

Jeremy Carl *Something*—I never do catch his surname, he re-
peats it so softly.

In these past weeks I've met a sizable number of truckers. One
brought along his wife and children; one looked like someone's
grandpa, gray-haired and hunchbacked and complaining of cold
in his chest. Another sported a black studded cowboy hat and
several tattoos. The youngest to pass through, bored and restless
during a previous stall, trashed the cab of his truck doing seventy

on an S-curve, "showing off," he explained, for the girlfriend he'd brought along for the ride.

Jeremy Carl Something is a more guarded sort. Blond hair tucked beneath a baseball cap, blue eyes covered by sunglasses, he pronounces wash "worsh" and resists our early efforts to draw him out. He seems content to spend his idle, waiting time staring toward the field in silence, but into our third stall of the day, we're not content to let him. Desperate for entertainment, we pester until he talks.

He starts by describing a few tricks of the trucker's trade: how to get a heavy load to market, back road style; how to get a license without filling out the paperwork. For a sentence or two he compares Carolina and Dakota potatoes and then, quite suddenly, as if the gears of speech only needed oiling, he's telling the grader crew more that we asked for, more than we needed to know, about his son, the woman who wouldn't stay faithful, a myriad of dead-end jobs and the nightmare of Vietnam.

He was "over there," he says, for seventeen months before he drove an Army truck over a land mine, killing his buddy and much of his own memory. He can't recall his captain's name but he remembers the Viet Cong's clever trick of sending water buffalo ahead of combat units to detonate enemy mines. He remembers the hellish climate, the stench of ditches filled with feces, and he remembers the happy-go-lucky fellow his buddy was and then was no more.

"I don't know if I ever thought about not going," he answers because I ask. "I don't know, but I don't think so."

The field truck that will cap Jeremy Carl's load and allow all of us to leave the dirt and noise and fierce mosquitoes for another day is on its way. The sky's too dark to track dust, so we track the reflection of headlights. The driver this go-around isn't Eddie Rose. While we finish grading, Eddie arrives with the rest of the digger crew, punches out and in his jacked-up, juiced-up pickup fishtails his way through the gravel parking lot onto open highway.

When the last of the potatoes drop off the boom, Jeremy Carl Something secures the cargo that has become his responsibility. With painstaking care he double-checks the locks and bolts of the back door, tests the running lights, records the hour of departure. Cautiously, very cautiously, he drives away from the grader canopy, slowly accelerating onto a highway Eddie Rose has already marked, driving forward into a much keener, much blacker night. But before he vanishes entirely, he waves goodbye with two fingers, the sign of peace.

When
Elvis Died

When I heard the report about Elvis—keeled over in his bathroom, the victim of a lethal combination of fourteen drugs— we were deep into flea and tick season in the American South, and I was driving to work at Greene Valley Kennels, owned and operated by Cindy Greene. When I arrived, Cindy too had heard the news. She greeted me at the door of her trailer in a Frederick's of Hollywood style nightie, pale-faced and red-eyed, her pet monkey hopping up and down behind her in a simulation of human distress.

"Did you hear? The King's gone."

Her husband, Owen, wanted to stay home from work as a show of respect, but his "bastard boss" wouldn't let him, she reported.

And so at Greene Valley Kennels the Elvis mourners were all women: Cindy, Paula the groomer, Shannon the pen keeper, and myself the clerk. Although Shannon postdated Elvis's major fame, she commiserated with the world's loss. Still a teenager, she had slipped out of Florida with her priest and now lived with him "in sin" in North Carolina. Timid with people, but excellent with animals, she let Paula and me handle the customers and customer relations. Large and imposing, Paula generally made short work of complaints and quibbles but our boss was harder to shut up. Once she simply had to say: "Not that it's any of your fucking business, Cindy, but when I leave this palace I writhe around on a waterbed just like you and Owen."

"Okay," Cindy shot back, undaunted, "but do you writhe with a *man?*"

In tribute, for the entire day, the local radio station played every great and not-so-great Elvis tune—"Hound Dog," "Teddy Bear," "You'll Never Walk Alone," "Suspicious Minds," "My Way." Somehow the voice held up during the body's transformation from jailhouse rocking mama's boy to beefy, drugged-out Nixon narc—no mean feat. Between answering the phone, blow-drying Afghans and scooping dog shit, we listened respectfully to that voice and felt genuinely sorry that it had departed.

Working for Cindy wasn't an entirely awful job. It only required the occasional perjury, primarily when health inspectors appeared in search of animals she bought and illegally transported across state lines. Her operation's piecemeal construction aided the deception. By the time the enforcers wound their way through the front room's stock of chain collars, pet beds and aquariums, past the grooming salon into the first maze of boarding cages, someone else had taken a short cut to the outside runs and transferred the big cats elsewhere. While I worked for her, Cindy acquired a tiger, a panther, a quarter horse, several exotic birds, the monkey and a litter of boxer puppies. Her house, lap and travel dog, however, was a silver toy poodle. Whenever she and Owen took off for the weekend, one of our jobs was to feed what remained of the menagerie.

Owen had been married once before to "the cow," as Cindy called her—a union that perplexed and irritated the successor to no end.

"She's ugly as all get out," she told us every other day. "God knows what he saw in her."

The product of that marriage, a son, came to visit one weekend a month. In her way, I suppose, Cindy made an effort ("I cooked every goddamn thing he wanted and still that little ass turned up his nose"), but she wasn't cut out for the role of stepmother or second wife. If Owen returned from work five minutes later that usual, she dove for the phone and double-checked his alibi.

Feet propped on the grooming tub, electric fan trained in her direction, she regaled us, her captive audience, with tales of romantic conquests, business coups and "life according to Cindy." If you disagreed on her take, the wisest course was to become mesmerized by the busy work of counting inventory or filling water bowls. She would argue a point until no one sane cared one way or the other.

When Cindy's sister Emma embarked on a sales career in copperware, we were required to attend the kickoff party at their mother's house. None of us wanted to go, but we did want to keep our jobs.

"And dress up!" our employer warned the three of us, clotted with dog and cat hair.

We all came in clean jeans and fairly clean tennis shoes to find our boss camouflaged by violent makeup, hair spray, earrings and a ruffled dress. The dull normality of her sister also startled us. Half the size of Cindy, she looked exquisitely delicate. You could imagine her sitting at a pink vanity, brushing her hair indefinitely. Even in her ruffle disguise, Cindy looked horsy, corralled in a den of fruit punch, sugar cookies and, of course, copperware.

After a product presentation, Emma discreetly distributed order blanks. Shannon, Paula and I discreetly ignored them until Cindy stomped over.

"So, what'll it be?"

The threat wasn't subtle. Even so, we had a hard time choosing. Kindly complimenting every pot, bowl and trinket, Shannon selected a miniature ashtray. In desperation Paula and I chose finger bowls.

"Good choice!" Cindy enthused, cheerful once we'd signed on the dotted line. "You can stick all sorts of shit in those finger things—rings, candy, Q tips, you name it."

The overall decor of Cindy's mother's house suggested the possibility of an Elvis altar on the premises: one of those assemblages that included vials of his sweat, strips of his bedsheets and a lighted portrait of the King that immortalized either the slim hips/sulky lips phase or the spangly girth of his jumpsuit era. On a bathroom run, I nosed around as best I could, but the only lighted portrait I found featured Cindy, dressed down in denim and kissing a horse.

At the end of my shift at Greene Valley Kennels, I freelanced as an onsite dog trainer for owners who could afford individual obedience instruction and avoid the chaos of mass classes. My afternoon client had purchased her black Labrador because she saw a woman jogging on the beach with a similar sidekick and liked the image, she said.

As time proved, she liked devoting thirty minutes to sit, heel and stay maneuvers far less. Often when I arrived, one of her two children met me at the door, trainer for the day. A case of too many handlers, too little consistency, and an understandably confused and rebellious dog. The program wasn't working and wouldn't, given the setup. Despite my sympathies for the animal, the day Elvis died I'd decided to leave a refund with whichever kid opened the door. Surprisingly, that afternoon the owner herself greeted me. The dog had run off again, she said, shrugging her shoulders, not too terribly concerned. Because he was wearing a tag, she expected the animal control unit to find and return him eventually. I didn't say the obvious: a tag could fall off. I kept my mouth shut; I also kept her money.

"At least have some coffee for your wasted trip," she offered.

In her crisp white kitchen, Mozart playing in the background, because I was tired or irked or maybe for the sheer hell of it, I introduced the jarring topic of Elvis.

She nodded vaguely; her secretary had mentioned his passing. A strange phenomenon, a truly odd character, she mused.

Arguing the merits of Elvis's appeal with her would have been as senseless as trying to out-holler Cindy Greene. More to the point, in that dog-abandoned house filled with European coffees and music, Elvis *was* rendered strange. Strange and entirely out of context.

Out of context myself and feeling it, I thought sourly: *Give the man some credit, bitch. Give a Cracker a break.*

Eye of
the Beheld

The body politic

The advertisement I answered requested females to model for two art classes during the university's summer session. A novice, I imagined standing still would be easy work, a summer job without sweat. It wasn't until much later that I heard a veteran nail the paradox. "Strangely enough," she said, "stillness is extremely taxing."

Exactly. Maintaining immobility, I sweated plenty.

For the drawing class, on a central platform, I held two-, five- and ten-minute poses. Shedding the robe for the first time, I wondered where to do it. On the platform or before I walked over—which looked less like a striptease and more like an ordinary step in a straightforward process? The instructor offered no clues. Once or twice he handed me a pole—to lift, not to lean against. It wasn't spectacularly heavy, but it was heavy enough. Within moments of holding it aloft, I felt the muscles in my arms cramp, prelude to a violent trembling throughout my body.

In the painting class I posed in a corner alongside a rusty tricycle, painted umbrella and gauzy curtains, one piece among many. I fainted my first day—not from heat or anxiety but from inhaling turpentine fumes. When I came to, the students were still painting. Probably they never stopped, accustomed to collapsing models.

I never called in sick, despite the trauma of dropping my robe before strangers, and eventually I stopped passing out from turpentine fumes. I adopted the blank, vacant stare everyone seemed to expect, fought off the fatigue of the sittings, didn't blush, didn't laugh, didn't cry. Outwardly I played the statue but all the while, inside, an internal voice railed on and on. Point One: nude spelled naked, no matter how highfalutin the presentation. Point Two: mine was the only bare ass in the room, just mine on display, not a stitch between me and the penetrating gaze of "the public." Although I could rebel against a background suspicious of plotless books and paintings that went beyond the scenic, apparently I couldn't escape its bullhorn.

Male pronouncements

While the rest of the drawing class disappeared on break for coffee or cigarettes, I stayed behind. At first I just sat, happy to rest my aching muscles, but once I realized no one, not even the over-achievers, returned before fifteen minutes had expired, I circled the room, inspecting the twenty-odd versions of myself.

"I thought I might as well stick to the idea that it's got two eyes, a mouth and a neck," Willem de Kooning said of his 1950s series *Women*.

A trace of German Expressionism in this slash of leg, a Cubist dismemberment here, a fairly realistic portrayal there, but none of the portraits resembled anyone I recognized. In them

I appeared as anonymous and interchangeable as I'd begun to feel while posing.

In *Matisse and Picasso*, Francoise Gilot described Matisse's models submitting to "endless sitting sessions, but as a result of *their good will and resilience* (my emphasis) they appeared in many canvases. . . ."

All of us in humid Carolina (not Paris) were beginners (not experts), and my resilience and good will were debatable. Even so, the Gilot observation applied: a model must derive her pleasure second hand, by inspiring—not creating—works of art.

Good will, resilience, beauty

I was fairly young but not at all thin when I modeled. The art department secretary hired me over the phone. No one suggested I come in for a once-over. At the time I thought that indicated a wonderfully egalitarian policy, but now I suspect a shortage of applicants accounted for the justice. That time of the month, another art department model made no bones about letting her tampon string dangle. On the basis of her example, one might assume confidence and body ease were also prime qualifications. But, again, when I applied, no one asked: "Can you handle this? Because if you run weeping from the room, you're going to leave us in a pickle."

Reubens might have liked his models plump, Shiele anorectic, Toulouse-Lautrec coarse, Ingres refined, but beauty, however quirkily defined, remained a model's calling card—beauty and youth. Jules Pascin demanded young, sensual models, most of them provided by his lover Lucy Krohg, according to Billy Kluver and Julie Martin in *Kiki's Paris*. If Krohg failed in that mission, Pascin was quick to carp: "Yesterday, a terrible procession of old biddies and wretches, too dirty to even want them for a maid. . . ."

Kiki herself (Alice Prin), a popular model during the 1920s and 1930s, felt so self-conscious about her "badly developed" pubic hair she filled in the skimpy parts with a black crayon before posing.

Always, there were standards. Pliny and Cicero told the tale of the stressed out painter Zeuxis, commissioned to decorate a temple with the perfect image of the perfect female, chagrined to find that none of the local beauties fit the bill. In the end he went with a composite approach. From this source the perfect knee, from that source the perfect nose.

"It is exactly like the fruit vendor," Picasso declared centuries later. "You want two breasts? Well, here you are, two breasts. . . ."

The model/lover

Although the Greeks preferred the male to the female form, by the Renaissance, if not earlier, nude portraits predominately featured females, and those portraits were painted predominately by males.

"I paint with my prick," said Renoir. "To paint a woman is to possess her," insisted Modigliani. "No nude, however abstract, should fail to arouse in the spectator some vestige of erotic feeling—and if it does not do so, it is bad art," warned critic Kenneth Clark. To pass on the chance of an erotic transfer from bed to canvas was to risk a mediocre career.

A few abstained from sleeping with their models, to be sure. But Dürer sounded less gallant than squeamish in his avoidance. "Don't let a woman live near you, don't touch any nude woman, guard against impurity," he shrieked.

The impurity angle didn't deter Picabia; he used another excuse. "The reason I don't paint models is that then I have to sleep with them and that tires me out."

Eventually someone did return early from a break and caught me snooping.

He wanted to know if I liked what I saw.

"Do you?" I asked, to avoid saying.

The canvas on the easel was "okay" in his judgment, but he had better sketches back at his apartment. Why didn't I come over and take a look? His invitation had nothing to do with seeing more of his work. He knew that, and I knew that. Yet my refusal smacked of hairsplitting. He'd seen me nude; in another two minutes he'd see me nude again. If he also took off his clothes, then we'd both be nude. What was a little thing like sex between two nude, consenting adults?

Well, what was it?

Non-erotic gratification

I received $10 an hour for my labor. Last year a model who worked at a museum in a decent-sized city told me she received the same. In Paris, around 1850, the going rate was four francs per four-hour sitting, although France Borel in *The Seduction of Venus* claimed very beautiful Jewish women could earn as much as six. When the French government deported Italian models as aliens without profession at the beginning of World War I, the Kikis filled in, young rebels who exchanged the lifestyle and stuffy morals of the provinces for romance and adventure in the big city.

And what did those rebels make of the Modiglianis who sang, giggled and mangled lines of poetry while they painted? What did their predecessors make of Degas, asking them to straddle a wash tub? Preserved reactions from the model front are scarce. Literature had to fill the gap.

The model as passive victim

In Zola's *The Work*, Christine becomes Claude's lover and official model. She poses for him, exhausts herself posing for him, and ultimately equates herself with a still life jug—no better, no more important. In Anne Walter's *Les relations d' incertitude,* the model describes a merger with the canvas, herself as "belonging" to the painter. In Joyce Cary's *The Horse's Mouth,* Gulley Jimson says of his model Sara: "I didn't know whether to draw her or bite her."

More often than not in "Life of the Artist" fables, after a bad art day, the protagonist vents his frustrations on the model, the closest scapegoat. By failing to inspire him, he feels, she colludes in his misery. In Walter's *Les relations d' incertitude,* the artist responds to that "betrayal" by jamming his paint brush into the model's vaginal "jug," then selling her to his buddies for sex.

I haven't yet come across its companion piece: a novel about a frustrated model sodomizing a painter with the tools of his trade, rampaging through his studio, destroying canvases, smearing paint.

But it's out there, somewhere. It must be.

Form without substance

I modeled on a few other occasions here and there, mostly for small groups in private art classes. Since I never posed for a single artist, I was never in a position to worry about a blocked painter attacking me. I quit, or thought I did, after turning blue posing for three hours in an unheated barn on Martha's Vineyard. It was time to quit. I'd proved I could disrobe before strangers with a studied casualness that implied a lack of Southern Baptist-tinged investment in the whole clothes shedding business.

Realistically I knew I'd never feel casual; the best I could hope for was an impression of nonchalance.

For my last job, the owner of an upstart mountain gallery hired me as part of his opening night extravaganza.

"It'll be a one-of-a-kind event," he bragged as we sat in the shell of a dilapidated storefront, discussing the possibilities. "Like nothing this town's ever seen."

"How much?" I asked.

"Thirty-five," he said.

"Okay," said I.

The exhibition showcased paintings by a local hairdresser and a wire cage full of animal/people. Three white striped females and two black striped males were already testing out growls and mock charges by the time I arrived debut night. The owner, decked out in suede boots and bolo tie, handed over my gear—a black, floor-length, voluminous cape and plastic face mask with eye slits. He pointed to a slightly raised box, somewhat larger than an oven, curtained on its fourth side in black. Once in the cape and mask, I was to climb in and stay put until he "gonged a bell," my cue to crawl out and slowly promenade as death's ominous stand-in.

I smiled a little then, who wouldn't have? But the fault was mainly mine. I hadn't checked out the specifics in advance. The artist wanted the model to kneel in the "altar/box" before the gong freed her to roam. Once I got behind the curtain, what the artist wanted held little sway, the problem being a lack of space to do much else except hunker down with my legs curled under me. I was still trying to negotiate the most comfortable position within those dimensions when the owner stripped the last of the brown paper from the glass front door, the caged models howled, and the show was on.

As much as possible I squirmed and reapportioned my weight, but very soon I couldn't feel my right leg below the knee. Guests meandered my way, sipping champagne and chewing munchies. "There's someone in there!" one exclaimed. (The curtain wasn't opaque.) My modeling comrades kept up quite a racket, but I suspected theirs was an overdrawn act. Probably no one had been paying attention to their fearsome antics for some time, but at least they got to move. I sorely envied them. My nerve endings bleated for mercy.

When my performance moment arrived and the gong rang out, the crowd instantly hushed. I'd waited long and desperately to hear that summons, but when it came, I couldn't make my limbs respond. Another gong: louder. Using my palms, I swiveled my butt outside the curtain. From there, I tried to step gracefully to the floor. I must have made contact but couldn't feel it. My right leg crumpled, and I, black robe and mask fell in a heap.

I expected titters, a gasp or two. The profound silence gave me the confidence to imagine the goof hadn't looked entirely like a goof in my camouflage outfit. I played the fall as part of the act, scurrying around on my hands and knees for a bit before using a ledge and my fingernails to pull myself up. I could walk, or hobble, as long as I dragged my right foot. So I dragged it, circling the room as instructed, doing my minute quota, clearing a path among the gawkers with my grimness, not a peep from any of them as I limped out the front door, heading for the alley and the gallery's back entrance.

Although Limping Death, in theory, manifests a kind of retro charm, the thirty-five bucks didn't cover my medical bills. Despite that, I considered the injury worth the chance to embody for an hour the ultimate form without substance. As a life model I showed my body and didn't speak; as Death I didn't speak and showed nothing, covered tip to toe.

"If I make a nude," Picasso said, "people should think that it is a nude, and not a nude of Mrs. So and So."

Ms. So and So

I admit I was slow on the uptake. Summer session was almost over before I understood that exposure in the model context abets dismissal. Revealing my anatomy got me treated as something a step below human and something far less sentient. Models perfect blankness; artists perfect indifference to the personalities that go along with those breasts, butts and bellies.

Over the course of art history, Ms. So and So has lost her arms, her feet, her head, her face. She's been depicted lounging, sleeping, silent, dead—a pliable, impassive object transformed by eye and brush, in service to talent.

But let there be no mistake, you artist-folk. You make of her, she makes of you. Eyes scan freely in an otherwise immobile body. While you're evaluating her lips, ankles and chin, judging her form and effort, she's also judging you. She's seen your tantrums, your grandiosities, your struggle. And down there in the trenches, she's seen you sweat.

Exchanging
Forever

Before turning twelve I attended more weddings than I have in the years since. Along with my mother, Shawboro women and most Shawboro men, I passed judgment on each bride on her wedding day. "If a woman doesn't look good on her wedding day," my mother would say and leave it at that, her follow-up sigh conveying the hopelessness of the unsaid.

The groom was mere backdrop. No matter how financially promising or handsome in his rented tux, he couldn't hold our interest. We'd gathered for the moment he, his ushers, the preacher and bridesmaids pivoted toward the vestibule where the star of the moment held onto her father's arm, too nervous or dazed or young to appreciate having brought the entire assembly to its feet, an accomplishment she couldn't reasonably expect to replicate.

Taking in the pageantry, I fantasized about my own bride's day—up to a point. The groom varied, depending on my current boyfriend, but the cast of bridesmaids remained fairly stable, a collection of cute (never steal-the-show pretty) friends and relatives. Poised to enter, a vision in white on my father's arm, I savored the crowd's attention, but after recording that supreme thrill my internal projector shut down. Even as a young girl I was disturbed by what lay beyond the step-slide toward public commitment: a father's abandonment at the altar, a mother's ragged sobs, solemn oaths that money and sickness wouldn't interfere with good humor or affection, declarations that only death would sever the bond, pledges to adhere to the absolutes of love, honor and fidelity.

In light of all that, why didn't every bride, in a fit of claustrophobic panic, turn and run toward fresh air and sunlight?

During my eleventh summer, my mother and I attended the nuptials of a couple who used the church bulletin to invite their guests. It was a small, sad affair. A single vase of droopy daisies decorated the church; one of my friends played the organ for free. She got through "Oh Promise Me" several times, waiting for the principals to enter. Whispers blamed the bride's family, habitually tardy. The majority of guests seemed primed for the scandal of a no-show, but following a very lengthy rendition of "I Love You Truly," the groom at last took his place beside the preacher, and we swiveled to see the bride, in a wrinkled suit trimmed with an inch or so of slip, give the nod for "Here Comes the Bride."

Her father hustled her down the aisle a tad too fast. Reciting what he'd recited a hundred times, the preacher stumbled. Throughout the ceremony the groom tugged at the short cuffs of his seersucker jacket. Refreshments served afterwards in the slightly mildewed Community Building were scant: a homemade layer cake, peanuts and a bowl of pink and green mints.

My mother tut-tutted. It was one of those occasions you believe you dismiss immediately and entirely once it ends. Yet of all the Providence Baptist unions, I remember most clearly the bride

of the rumpled suit and hanging slip, how genuinely she celebrated despite a lack of enthusiasm all around.

Of my childhood friends, the organist married first and elsewhere. Soon after her eighteenth birthday, she eloped. At the
time I was devastated that she'd foregone a trip down the aisle
of Providence Baptist—I'd hoped to be a cute (not pretty) satel-
lite to her star.

My last year of high school I received a letter from Linda at
college, asking me to be her maid of honor. A small wedding, at
home, she said. Just the family. I hadn't known she'd been dating
anyone seriously, much less considering marriage, but of course I
accepted. She wore an A-line sheath of yellow linen she'd sewn
herself and I wore a horrible two-piece frilly number, pale blue
with white flowers. I stood at her side before the preacher, in front
of a mantle decorated with magnolia branches from a tree she
and I first scaled twelve years before. My hand shook handing over
the ring; her husband's voice shook saying "I do", but Linda remained completely unruffled and took the entire life-altering
event in stride.

The weddings I attended during my college years were de-
signed to deviate—flagrantly and militantly—from hometown
fare. One took place at twilight in a stone amphitheatre. The
bride and groom included a phrase of pillow talk in their vows. In
conclusion, everyone sang a Cat Stevens's tune and several males
unashamedly and rather pointedly wept. Another college bride
was "given away" to her third husband by her second in a "ceremony of love and forgiveness." Carnivores were out of luck at
the wedding dinner served afterwards in the bride's stepfather's
pagoda-inspired home—not a sliver of meat in sight. At a third
celebration, the Catholic priest presiding enjoined guests to

become part of an "aura of love" by turning toward the nearest stranger and "connecting." The three Polish carpenters flown in from the mother country to build a reception balcony missed much of that ceremony's nuance. Many a native son and daughter missed the nuance, myself included, but the balcony was an arresting piece of handiwork and well stocked with booze.

After years of the unconventional, I was amazed to hear that McGuire, dormmate and apartment-mate, had opted for the whole traditional shebang: engraved wedding announcements, bridal showers, flower girls, ring bearers, soloists, something old, something new, something blue. Our mutual friend Brenda called to confirm the news. Was it possible? Could this be? After a long, self-imposed hiatus, Brenda once again kept company with men but, like me, remained suspicious of binding legal contracts. The two of us mocked and howled at McGuire's lapse in judgment and agreed to travel together to West Jefferson with our doubts and raised eyebrows.

We arrived late at the bridal shower, but the bride-to-be, mother of the bride, mother of the groom and assorted others, all of whom greeted us at the door in a wave of good cheer and converging colognes, had waited for us to open the gifts. In a living room of embroidered pillows, graduation portraits and chintz, Brenda and I retreated to the piano stool with our teensy wedges of cake and settled between ourselves that the worst had certainly occurred: McGuire was eating this crap up! Like a veteran she oohed and aahed over each present, profusely thankful. More to the point, she seemed actually *pleased* with the toaster covers and hand-painted bells.

"So are you going to keep the name McGuire or what?" Brenda blurted.

The pending mother-in-law cleared her throat; the bride's mother shoved a new gift into her daughter's lap. Brenda grew up Southern. She knew the rules of delicacy and decorum, knew all about busy-beaver, phlegm-hawking warnings. But at that particular juncture Brenda wasn't interested in warnings or delicacy or decorum and neither was I. We wanted the facts. Was McGuire to be vanquished—yes or no?

The bride took her time answering—unbullyable. On the front page of the dissertation, on conference papers, on journal submissions, McGuire would stand. On checks, driver's license and income tax forms, McGuire would succumb to Sandling.

It wasn't the answer we'd hoped for. Sure, McGuire was her father's name, as patriarchal in origin as Sandling. But it was also the name by which she'd been identified for twenty-six years. By dint of long-term use, we figured she'd made that title her own.

After the bridal shower, we attended the wedding rehearsal, and after the rehearsal, the rehearsal dinner, held in a family-style restaurant on the outskirts of town. From the groom's camp came jokes about his Army days. The brides' relatives worked God into their well-wishing. Brenda and I grumbled to each other and waited for someone to pay sly homage to the couple's inventiveness during their previous year of secret cohabitation. Depending on which set of parents visited, the storage basement of their apartment building filled with stereo equipment, Jockey underwear and shaving lotion or skis, electric curlers, and Tampax. I thought Brenda might contribute a veiled reference to the dermatologist-supplied birth control pills; she must have counted on my guile. In the end, neither of us rose to offer revelations or congratulations. We'd entered the speechless zone.

Still, I held out hope. At the church, seated in the sanctuary and waiting for the beginning of McGuire's step-slide, I devised a plan whereby she could yet escape her predicament, honor intact.

When the minister solicited objections, admonishing all who failed to speak to forever hold their peace, several hands would shoot up at once. Well-delivered, persuasive arguments regarding the fallibility of love and the unreasonableness of monogamy would gain credence with each new promoter. The caring parents would decide to overlook the vast monetary outlay in favor of their children's sanity. Finally the on-hold bride and groom would speak, admitting that God and state were unnecessary complications to their private bond of love.

As I sank deeper and deeper into that daydream, the real ceremony got underway. The ushers wore dark green tuxedos, accented by paler green cummerbunds. The soloist who performed "Here, There and Everywhere" also wore green—a sweeping, scoop-necked dress of velveteen. By the time the groom in white stood ready to receive his bride in white, I'd regenerated the panic associated with every first step toward a husband and away from an open door.

When I finally married, I avoided a church setting, my skittishness and claustrophobia and fear of vanishing sunlight too well ingrained by then. I knew I couldn't finish a walk down any aisle.

Our tardy ceremony took place beneath blooming dogwoods in my brother's yard. McGuire and Brenda attended, as did my immediate family, but the majority of guests were friends of my husband-to-be. A woman minister performed the rites. Since we hadn't met with her beforehand, she suggested the three of us duck into a bedroom for an impromptu "practice." In a clump between beds, we took turns reciting, reflected in a slightly disfiguring mirror, surrounded by pictures of my brother and Jane on their wedding day.

At my insistence, guests were served champagne as soon as they arrived. I needed to drink pre-event and couldn't very well drink alone. An hour passed, then another. Ostensibly, we were waiting for two of the missing—waiting and drinking. But finally, all accounted for, no legitimate excuses for stalling left, the ritual began. As bride and groom we lined up in front of the minister, my family alongside us. When my mother emitted one brief gasping sob, both my father and brother sidestepped to shield me from the distraction of her contorted face. I said what I had to say, he said what he had to say, the minister said what the state required, and afterwards we served ourselves deli sandwiches from a buffet table and more champagne.

Balancing a plateload of salami and smiling, the minister sidled in close to offer congratulations. And then, for no reason I've ever been able to understand, she said: "You know, technically, after the bedroom session, you were already married." I must have blanched because she reached out with her free hand and touched my shoulder with some concern. Foolish me. I'd assumed a rehearsal was a rehearsal, not the real McCoy. I'd assumed, in that bedroom, I still had time to flee.

Once the guests departed, my new husband departed too, for our house. I stayed on at my brother's, helping to clean up the rubble in my $50 wedding dress, grass-stained along the hem and champagne-dribbled down the bodice. I'd been drunk for most of the afternoon and looked drunk, but I didn't feel drunk. I felt disoriented and weirdly allergic.

Less than three hours into forever, I'd broken out in hives.

The
Coupling
and the Un

I heard the following tale about two of the mismatched who married from several sources. She taught architecture; he studied computer science. Most of the drama took place in Pittsburgh, but other locales were also involved: Paris, a river. It starts off as one of those academic-circle attractions, but with a twist. Instead of the brilliant older male seducing the beautiful younger female, a beautiful younger male was seduced by a brilliant older female. In time, to cement her hold, the brilliant convinced the beautiful he wasn't so beautiful after all, not even ordinarily attractive. She chose her spot of vulnerability well. Since he'd accepted his mental mediocrity, he counted on his looks.

When he finished his degree, they married, announced her pregnancy and moved to Paris. Within the year they returned to Pittsburgh, childless. She insisted he go on a diet, which he did, losing (in the opinion of friends) pounds and luster. He was seen vacuuming university hallways with his own personal machine. Several weeks later, she reported him missing. Divers recovered his body from the river. Evidence suggested a leap from the bridge. Fish had fed on him.

Her subsequent interviews with police were odd, hysterical sessions. The diet had ruined his looks, she said, gesturing toward a wall covered with nude photographs. "He used to be so lovely." She called a press conference to describe her "personal ordeal." They had been planning to design "cities of the future" together; now she must go that route alone.

She told one, possibly two, the story of their last night together. As retold to a wider audience: the two were in bed, asleep, when he woke and bellowed: "I hate computers; I hate Pittsburgh; and I hate you." Then he left the apartment, presumably en route to the river.

I was living in Provincetown when the first of my brother's marriages began to fray—a dignified, cordial unraveling, no accusations or counter-accusations, an amicable division of property and goods. The news seemed to upset me far more than either of the principals. I thought my brother had made a perfect match— the first time around.

When his second bride called to fill me in on "her side of the breakup," I asked not to hear it. And I didn't, really. Mostly I heard a checklist of my brother's faults: a wildly over the top account even a nonrelation would have found suspect. I wanted to laugh, and I would have laughed if the shrew on the phone hadn't been married to someone I loved.

"Your brother has always been a romantic," our mother once declared, neither pleased nor approving. By that she meant: your brother can be yanked around. You, you make mistakes, but at least you're *practical.* At least you don't get *carried away.*

The very day I called from another state to suggest divorce, my husband of record canceled my credit card and closed our joint bank account. At the time, I carried two twenties and a ten in my wallet, the last of the available funds. I could have asked for a parental loan, but I had that reputation of practicality to preserve. Show me the practical woman who calls long distance to ask for a divorce holding fifty bucks.

In a jam I took a job at a summer camp in western New York. The director never tired of fishing for the "real reason" behind my bewildering acceptance of a $500 salary, plus six weeks room and board. I was the oldest counselor he'd ever hired.

"I've never been a camp counselor," I hedged.

("Yeah, so?")

"It's a long, boring story."

("Yeah, so?")

"I'm in the middle of a divorce."

("A *divorce*! You mean you're *married*????")

I was assigned the eight- to eleven-year-old girl bunk. One of the other counselors, Debbie, had been either a camper or a counselor every summer of her life since the age of five. A poster girl for "can-do" spirit, she owned a dozen Camper-of-the-Year awards. I liked Debbie; she had a good heart and always corrected my gaffes kindly. But the saving grace of the summer was Anna. Twenty-two going on eighty, feisty, red-haired Anna started mouthing off during a counselor trust exercise, and the teammate she was supposed to catch leaned back and fell through the hole.

On Parents' Day, the cars began to stream through the gates before breakfast. Large and small cars but all uniformly expensive. The *de rigueur* outfit of the day was denim, accessorized with a lot of gold. Current husbands and wives were often related to more than one set of campers. Step-lineage grew complicated to trace. Asked to clarify, the kids usually did so in an offhanded, exceedingly worldly way. ("Yeah, my dad was once married to Tracy's mom.")

Laura and Steffie, current step-sisters, might have waltzed out of a fairy tale. Blond, gabby and popular, Laura had straight teeth and the beginnings of a chest. Knobby, raven-haired Stef sported a mouthful of metal. Although Steffie started out in Laura's bunk, that arrangement hadn't worked out. Tall for her age but naive, she soon became the bunk's whipping post. When she transferred to our younger bunk, her height isolated her all the more. She spent the night before Parents' Day packing her trunk.

When Steffie's Dad and Laura's mom saw the trunk, they blamed her counselors. She'd stayed all summer last summer. How hard could it be to keep a kid entertained for six weeks? We had two choices, Steffie's father informed us: convince his daughter to stay or forfeit our end-of-summer tips.

"But, Dad, I want to come home," Steffie pleaded from her trunk seat.

"We're leaving for British Columbia next week ourselves," Laura's mother objected. "What would you do at home?"

"Steffie, this is *very* bad timing," her father seethed.

"Maybe you're not trying hard enough," her step-mother resumed. "I just talked to Laura, and she says this year's been loads of fun."

At that, a weeping Steffie fled the room.

I chose my next job, counting and ordering lingerie for a chain of New England discount stores, for the flexible hours and travel opportunities. (Anna signed on to run a program for street kids in Boston. "Delinquents, princesses," she said. "Six of one, half dozen of the other.")

One of the advantages of a road job is that it allows you to keep in touch with rather far flung friends. When Ingrid threw a surprise birthday party for her husband, Bruce, in their Hartford studio, I knocked off early and helped Ingrid and her mother-in-law hang the balloons and crepe paper. Someone was waylaying the birthday boy elsewhere until five. Ten minutes or so before his arrival, I met a belly dancer in the bathroom, veiling herself in chiffon. An enterprising sort, she handed over her agency's brochure which advertised belly dancing telegrams and "man-grams." For a few bucks extra, special messages could be scrawled across "the belly or shoulders" of a "lovely" or "handsome" performer. An "Arabian Fantasy Party," the most expensive option on the list, featured a mixture of male and female performers who danced, served dinner, "fanned guests" and fed grapes from the stalk to one and all.

I assumed Ingrid had hired her.

When Leila the belly dancer undulated into the party, Bruce was sitting on a folding chair in the middle of the room. He giggled sheepishly but his mother guffawed.

Leila's dance seemed to last longer than five minutes, although it probably lasted less than fifteen. But even five minutes is a long time to watch someone gum grapes. Bruce laughed louder as the performance continued, but only his mother laughed steadily start to finish.

As did ours, Ingrid's reaction fluctuated. Her position was exceedingly tricky. If she chose protest, she risked being labeled a prude, a no-fun type gal; she risked her husband siding with his mother against her, a pattern no wife wants to encourage. Yet a ringing endorsement seemed hardly appropriate either. In any event, it didn't come off. Her attempts at smiling, laughing and clapping were painful to watch. In her heart of hearts she may have been enraged, but on the surface she looked primarily hurt. Was that the mother-in-law's dual intent? To amuse her son and humiliate his wife, still puffy from her last pregnancy, in no shape to appear in a hip-hugging skirt of chiffon?

Hard to say.

I watched for clues—a gloating glance from the mother-in-law, a tense, whispered exchange between husband and wife, but saw neither. The sequence of birthday events proceeded: gifts, toasts, cake and ice cream.

But once we cleared out, once the cake had been eaten, the champagne drunk, the presents loaded into the Volvo, during that long drive home, what passed between Ingrid and Bruce? Did the belly-dancing incident count as nothing, a minor disagreement or did it form the festering core of a long-term grudge?

I know that Bruce and Ingrid didn't officially divorce, but what does any outsider really know about the bond between couples? Maybe their relationship remained rock solid. Maybe it was the work of glue. Maybe, all along, it was pure facade.

Someone Else's City

The guy who rents the first floor apartment dyed his hair blue, the same shade of blue he painted his apartment walls. His name is common enough, but the name he goes by is Belgian Zohr. He moved to New York from Hawaii and currently sells one-of-a-kind costumes to an art gallery in Soho. Last week he broke the lock on the building's thermostat and set the temperature to emulate the tropics. Afterwards the landlord threatened to evict Belgian and his roommate, a writer of surrealistic fiction. The roommate has been feeling fragile and suicidal of late, Belgian reports. For two weeks he's worn his bathrobe inside out all day.

Belgian ignores the eviction threat from Richard, our artist-landlord, because a family long threatened with removal remains in residence on the second floor. They date from a time, pre-Richard, when the building housed struggling welfare recipients, not struggling artists. For cash the man of the family sells stolen bicycles. He advertises by riding his stock on the Williamsburg streets, occasionally striking a deal with the Hasidim. I've never seen the woman he lives with (quite possibly his wife) on a ten-speed, but she often sits on the floor of the second landing, asking if anyone has spotted Richard.

The top floor of the building is hotter, also quieter. Between subway and doorway, there are six city blocks, a Kung Fu theatre, a burnt-out pizzeria, a sad corner Woolworth's, a laundromat filled with bucolic calendars, a canine corpse hung from a street lamp, a motorcycle gang and their headquarters. My own territorial impositions include white walls and hearty ivy. My fire escape offers a view of the Williamsburg Bridge, prettier at night when both the bridge and East River sparkle. The superiority of night sightseeing works to my advantage since in New York I can't afford the luxury of sleeping in.

Shirley, on East 71st, can. Her time is financed by relatives eager to have a Ph.D. in the family. Her apartment near the park is small, clean, exorbitantly priced and reasonably safe from all intruders save the cockroach. A painting of General Robert E. Lee hangs above the dining table; the potting soil, shipped from North Carolina, is guaranteed to grow anything, anywhere, even in a certifiably "Yankee" outpost. At the end of our weekly visits, I take the Lexington line to Canal Street and there, in the hollowed-out tunnel, wait for the Jamaica Plains J train: dry-mouthed, my heart in a clinch.

That I still react to fear, amusement or pity on the streets or in the subways amuses Anson, another friend who specializes in the production of black cloth boxes.

"A momentary maladjustment," he says of my affliction. "You'll get used to the jitters along with the puke and the dog shit."

The stance suits him. In Tribeca he pinned his mugger to the sidewalk and kept him pinned until the police arrived. During the scuffle he broke one finger and cracked several ribs but decided not to press charges when he heard he counted as the kid's first offense. The morning Anson found a derelict sharing his accommodations, he emptied the man's pockets before tossing him out. Anson has New York Savvy. Not generic savvy but the particular strain indigenous to New Yorkers, the kind I am without.

The failing exasperates one of my part-time employers, the wife of a New Church minister. Not only do I lack New York Savvy, she intimates I lack New York Spirit as well when I announce plans to sit out the subway strike. From the director's office at the museum, where I also work part time, no one bothers to call and question my absence. I'm strictly fluff there, typing an occasional interdepartmental memo, hand delivering a letter from the executive offices to the curator of European Paintings. Any such errand could include a full museum tour because not only am I part time, I'm temporary. And temporary employees aren't required to be responsible, efficient or particularly polite.

On the TV news, I watch crowds of spirited New Yorkers getting to work regardless, trying to locate that speck on the screen that would be Pam, assistant to the executive assistant to the museum's director. After being snatched off her bicycle near Times Square, she decided to jog to work, which she does whether or not the subways are operating. Within the executive offices, Pam's desk is separated from mine by a glass partition— an illusion of privacy in an office where none exists. The week the director was vacationing in Paris, his executive assistant vacationing in Ohio, business was slow enough to accept personal calls.

If he called again, I overheard her warn, she'd have him arrested. Had she made herself perfectly clear?

The caller, her boyfriend, periodically fell victim to psychotic episodes. He'd fallen victim the night before, gutting her mattress with one of her sharper kitchen knives. She only threatened to call the police when a full night's sleep became essential, she explained, possibly because I was staring. Rested, she found his company exciting.

When not eating pizza or scanning the TV, I pace. If I fall asleep, I have trouble waking. To Shirley, Strike Day Eleven, I describe what is immediately understood.

"Restless as a chinch," she says.

Restless as a chinch.

For eleven consecutive nights I've studied the vacant, nine-storied factory across the street. From dusk till dawn six of the nine floors stay lighted. Between 3 and 4 A.M. the motorcycle gang returns. After a few desultory revvings they too close up shop, the street then as empty as it gets, as empty as the bombed out buildings on either side.

In the building beside mine, from a bedroom I could, if I roused myself, peer into, I hear a deep voice accusing, a high voice denying. The first breakable object sails through their window and crashes in the street. The second, a whiskey bottle, clears their window and mine. What form is left to the glass rolls along my floorboards and into a corner. I'm almost sorry when it stops. In a city of eight million, silence is the perversion.

By Day Fourteen I can subway to work lacking both savvy and spirit but not, of course, the fare, soon to be raised according to the newly negotiated contract. Nonetheless, for the time being, all remains unaltered—except at the ticket counter of the museum's Egyptian entrance, where a writer I met in Province-town, with two books on his résumé, is making change of a twenty.

"For the contact," he explains when I ask. "Come down at lunch. We'll talk."

But at lunch he's tethered to the pay phone, on long-term hold. Since last we communicated he's fallen in and somewhat out of love with a nineteen-year-old from Denver; just now, her pre-twenty problems are starting to grate.

But what about me and my adventures in the big city?

I can't quite manage a thirty-second reply.

He speaks into the receiver. I point to my watch, mouthing "gotta go." He holds up a "wait a second" finger, following along, stretching the cord.

Will I be at Myron's opening? We can catch up there.

Absolutely, I say.

Super, says he.

The cord has stretched its limit.

At five o'clock it's raining, harder across the river at Marcy Avenue.

"Terrible day, isn't it?" a stranger and fellow pedestrian asks, innocuously enough.

He has a forgettable face, slightly nasal voice. He bets I'm an artist. A painter, right? He knows lots of "them." See lots of "them" at parties all the time. But he hasn't seen me. Did I just move? To Broadway? Where exactly do I live?

Since he's keeping up with a walk that verges on a run, his pronouncement that I must be one of those art farts too good for the general populace comes breathless. When I dart toward the car attendant at Peter Luger's, my inquisitor surprises me by charging even faster ahead, around the corner and out of sight.

For a moment I hesitate. The rain shows no sign of letting up, I'm running late, and the route around the edge of the defunct Brooklyn Shipyard will take awhile. Still, there are fewer blind alleys in that direction, more open space for sprinting. Weighing my options, I eventually decide that getting soaked is the least harmful outcome. Unlike other kinds of damage, in time, rain will evaporate.

By nine, the weather has cleared, and a fair number of Provincetown folks have gathered at the Whitney. Kissing the guest of honor is necessary and time consuming, given the line. He reaches out, I reach out; we brush cheeks although, truly, we don't know each other. Rather: I know someone who knows him, and he knows someone who is fond of me. There is quite a bit of brush-the-cheek kissing, very little drinking (since the drinks aren't free) and even less art previewing (since the art is over-whelmed by the number of guests). I've already un-checked my coat when the ticket taker/writer arrives. We wave, too far apart to kiss.

The executive assistant herself calls to say the museum has run out of temporary funds and can't afford me. She's sorry, she says, and she's very nice to have delivered the news herself. She could have handed the ax to manic Anthony, my job seeker at Network Temps.

"Tough break about the museum, kid," he says at our subsequent ten o'clock appointment. "But we'll fix you up. Sixty-five a minute, right? No problem."

Back in the reception area, I wait beside a woman surreptitiously eating chocolates, bending over a pocketbook cache. Between incessant incoming calls, the receptionist offers coffee all around.

"I didn't come for coffee," a thin black woman reprimands. "I came for a job, understand?"

"Sweetheart, sweetheart."

Anthony is paging the secret eater of chocolates. He's on the phone; he believes he has something. When she rises, the chair creaks.

I'm the next sweetheart beckoned.

"A plum," he says, speaking of the job. "Didn't I tell you?" he asks, speaking of faith. "Any problems, just dial," he concludes, scribbling an address off Wall Street on his multipurpose pad.

The woman who refused coffee doesn't give him a chance to beckon. As I turn, she's already charging his desk.

From the twenty-second floor of a skyscraper, the angle changes. A mosaic of roof tops, countless glass windows, infinite pavement, movement so minimal it barely deserves the title. No noise, no smells, no ugliness. Even if you happened to glimpse a beating, mugging or murder, the distance between you and the violence would relieve you of the burden of Samaritan intervention.

Another corporate perk.

Here I can take any number of breaks to assess the view because my boss for the day is on his way out of the corporation. By week's end, he'll no longer be vice president of his division at Paine Webber or entitled to a Paine Webber secretary, however temporary.

All morning long his phone has rung twice. Besides taking messages, I take in the view and wait for five o'clock. The on-notice VP is personable, fiftyish, a believer in the phrases: "I'm going to give things a little more time" and "I'm going to keep my options open." He prefers the description "conflicting interests" to "fired."

When he returns from lunch at the Princeton Club, he's holding a birthday card for his wife. He wants to know what I think of his choice and we try to talk long and hard about birthday sentiments because bereft of conversation he fights the panic badly: a tightness runs down his jaw and captures his lower lip. After greeting cards we discuss my interests. He has an uncle in publishing, he exclaims. Once upon a time he'd considered the profession himself. I must call his uncle; I must. Slipping me a name and number, he assures me connections are the ticket in this town.

"Believe me, I know," he says.

I do.

If you allow yourself to be waylaid from the purpose of flight, even momentarily, the five o'clock rush will overtake you. To get around and between the crush of bodies, the elbow in the ribs, the alien breath, to endure the slamming shut, the pitching forward, the endlessness of transport, blankness must be perfected, a blankness impervious to all grades of human suffering. For three days now I've passed the same man, sitting in his urine, conversing with someone who doesn't exist or perhaps with someone who refuses to respond, like me.

On South 8th Street, the motorcycle gang has gathered early for engine repair.

"Let the lady through, man," the leader orders, flipping back his braid.

"Thanks," I say, flipping back mine.

There's fresh graffiti on the outside door, two letters in my rusty box. Anson is throwing another potluck dinner party on Friday; the other bears a Carolina postmark.

"Long time no hear," it reads.

True. I can't remember the last time I saw this person, much less corresponded. She's curious: what *am* I doing in such a godforsaken place? Even in print, the question reverberates mystification. Am I researching perverts? Writing bizarro fiction? Her first-paragraph queries aim at funny. The entire letter aims at funny and misses.

At Anson's last potluck gathering, deserters from the Mudd Club crashed the fun, and at 5 A.M. Anson found a woman he didn't know, nursing a baby he couldn't recognize, on his bed. The next morning one of his black boxes had been slit, and his friend's sea turtle painting had been smeared. "A pisser," he said, but minimal damage, considering the wall to wall freakout.

Friday's crowd, at the onset, appears mellower: ten of us surrounded by 4,000 square feet of loft space. Shower, sink and toilet Anson installed himself (illegally). Illegally he'll charge the next tenant a fixture fee for his labors and make a bundle, he says. However, cashing in and relocating are both on hold as of last week when Anson's newest girlfriend transferred herself, cat and artwork to this address. Tonight she's deep in conversation with a painter of metallic flowers. Her final enthusiastic critique: "Definitely New Wave."

Around the table where the food should be, the topic is teaching. The teaching of art. WHY TEACHING ART IS GOOD, POSSIBLY THE BEST VEHICLE, FOR CONFIRMING ONE'S ARTISTIC DIRECTION. This defense comes from a man clothed in Mickey Mouse t-shirt and matching baseball cap.

At the table sits someone I know slightly better than the others, someone I once considered a sly wit. While the pedagogue argues that his second profession is AT LEAST AS SACRED AS THE CREATION OF ART, the comedian rhythmically flicks a cigarette lighter open and shut, edging the flame closer and closer to his face. Eventually the yellow shoots up and singes an eyebrow, and for a few moments he puts the lighter away. If he felt content with singing one eyebrow, maybe I wouldn't have decided. But soon the lighter returns for an encore—my cue to move on.

The minister's wife says I never suited New York and New York never suited me. From the beginning she inferred as much.

"Didn't I, ducky?" she quizzes the minister, dressed for his afternoon stroll. "Didn't I always say she and New York didn't mix?"

He crosses his gloved hands and wanly smiles.

"It is not a city for the mediocre. For those it shows no pity."

He seems pleased with the cadence. Perhaps the next New Church secretary will be typing that opinion.

His wife sighs deeply. "You were so good with the mimeograph machine. Not everyone is, you know. It's very old, *very* temperamental."

I stop stapling sermons long enough to assure her she'll no doubt find an excellent replacement, someone whose typing and mimeographing skills will put mine to shame. This is, after all, New York.

For a moment she seems to consider the likelihood, but when the stapling resumes, she disagrees.

The market's against her; everything conspires against her these days.

I repeat my confidence that such is not the case.

"Oh most certainly it is the case," she corrects.

Surely not.

"Oh yes," she says. "Yes."

In the two weeks I give myself to be the tourist I always was, despite the illusion of permanent domicile, I contemplate dinosaur bones and take the Red Line Cruise around Manhattan for a closer look at the green Lady of Liberty. I eat street hot dogs for breakfast, street pretzels for lunch. At night I have a choice: every movie playing in America is playing somewhere in the city.

Shirley, still on 71st, has devised one last-ditch scheme to keep me here. I should abandon Brooklyn for Manhattan, find challenging employment and allow her to introduce me to a barrage of eligible males. Until locating something better, I can bunk with her and General Lee.

Annoyed by yet another refusal, she lets slip a startling new warning.

"You're going to be bored, you know. Once you've lived in New York, everywhere else will bore you stiff."

She may well have a point. The inverse is certainly true. Within the circumference of the place I've never felt bored. I've never felt at ease.

Live,
Onstage

The first time I escaped home for any extended period of time I attended Governor's School, a state-funded program housed at Salem College. Along with 399 other North Carolina high school students, for two months of the summer of 1968, I participated in an educational experiment that emphasized the very latest in cultural doctrines and ideological trends. In our English class, we discussed George Harrison lyrics as poetry and produced a film in which no one spoke but everyone dressed in raincoats and bounced balls repetitively in doorways to symbolize stagnant life. Since I'd never been near a motion-picture camera or discussed as opposed to memorizing anything poetic, I was thrilled with the curriculum. But it built on no foundation in my case. Seventeenth, fifteenth or twentieth century trends—they were all new terrain for me.

For those two months I lived in such a taut state of hyper-awareness that I lost sleep, ten pounds and a menstrual period. During lunch I stayed in my dorm room, frantically transcribing all that I could remember from the morning sessions, loath to forget a single revelation. The dorm mother assumed I was pregnant after I fainted at an outdoor concert and was carried (they tell me) by two guys to the refreshment stand and revived with Dr. Pepper. After the concert she marched me over to the infirmary for a going-over by the nurse.

"I'm fine, really," I kept assuring them both, but *fine* didn't quite describe my circumstance. Alert, absorbent, enthralled maybe—but *fine* implied a state of equilibrium that didn't apply. I was wide-open and jazzed but not for sex, a distinction lost on the nurse and dorm mother. Hoisted on the examining table, I wish I could have said: "Sex is a revolt of the body, ladies; it's my mind that's fled the convent."

I'd just heard an adult declare GOD IS DEAD without being fried on the spot. How could fooling around compare?

In the mornings we met according to disciplines; in the afternoons, as a group, we heard lectures on art, music and philosophy. At night we attended concerts and dance recitals. Heady stuff all, but none headier for me than live theatre. In eight weeks we saw eight plays, the first a scrappy production of Peter Weiss's *The Persecution and Assassination of Marat as Performed by the Inmates of the Asylum of Charenton under the Direction of the Marquis de Sade.*

As we waited in our matinee seats for the nonexistent curtain to rise, an exaggerated pattern of light and shadow rolled over us—blatantly artificial, yet so eerily evocative of dream lighting that, as with dream, the effect felt both familiar and tantalizingly askew. After a moment of total blackness, the lights went up onstage and "inmates" poured from the wings, drooling, jabbering and slapping themselves. The theatre was small and intimate enough to see the twitchy fingers, soiled costumes and trowel makeup from every seat. Marat's bath occupied center stage. I remember the tub, the actor's spotlighted languor, the white bandage circling his forehead, his convincingly pasty skin, his tranquility among the chaos. I remember the disturbing specter of the sleep-walking Charlotte and the obsessed Duperret, grabbing at that ghost whenever she passed. Most vividly I remember the wild-eyed insane and their periodic, piercing shrieks.

Jean Paul Marat's politics, Charlotte Corday's guillotine end, the infamous specifics of Sade's claim to fame—historical references and ironies, I missed them every one. But my ignorance was also a plus. It allowed me to focus entirely on the rebellion onstage. When the actors squealed, I flinched; when they charged, I cringed. I didn't tap into the "message" of anarchy and madness; I tapped into the spectacle. Armed with a critical perspective, I'd have felt much safer in my seat. As it was, I felt infinitely in danger of being yanked into the bedlam, drooled on, grabbed at, cursed and mocked. When Coulmier and his family decamped and the inmates rushed willy-nilly into the aisles, I was terrified. By the time the "stage manager" blew his whistle and the actors, suddenly calm, swiveled toward the audience to clap at us, I'd visited every cubbyhole of my paranoia, and the experience left me limp with fatigue.

Deeply spoiled by my Governor's School adventures, I returned home, restless and dissatisfied with almost everything about high school. One of the few exceptions was the senior class play, inaugurated that year by my English teacher, Dorothy Hess. For some crazy, great reason, she decided to direct a farce about mix and match identities with an awful title (*The Adorable Imp*). Anyone could audition, but she had already settled on who would play which role and made no attempt to conceal those irreversible decisions, a director/dictator from the start.

For several exhilarating weeks we rehearsed after school in a musty auditorium. Every afternoon from a different seat in a different row of that echo chamber, Mrs. Hess screeched: "Louder! I can't hear you!"

By performance time, we screeched also.

When the cast came down with a nasty case of stage fright the week before opening night, Mrs. Hess arranged a preview show for the grammar school kids to settle our nerves. There were three of us onstage, zipping along, happily screeching our lines, when suddenly my "stage mother" drew a blank. The "maid" and I stared breathlessly, waiting for her to recover. Then we tried backtracking, repeating our lines, repeating her lines, to jog her memory. Nothing worked. Where was the *prompter*? Where was *Mrs. Hess*? Up there in the spotlight the tension was terrific and terrible. The unscripted silence dragged on and on, dragging us with it. And then as suddenly as the blip occurred, the connection was restored. Mom recalled her speech, barked it and we lurched on.

Still, the gap left its mark. For the rest of the performance, we garbled whole paragraphs in our hurry, the banshee of silence nipping at our heels.

If I hadn't written myself into a corner, trying to bring off a short story with too many characters at a single-set dinner party, I wouldn't have tried to convert fiction into drama. At the onset, my cache of rationalizations seemed convincing. In play form, I could rid the piece of all those annoying, distracting "Gay said, Frank said, Jessica said" tags. And the script did get rid of internal ID; that much, it accomplished.

The company that produced my effort was located in another state, too far away for me to attend rehearsals, so the director called in his questions and concerns.

"We're just not one hundred percent sold on that line," he'd say. Or: "We want to insert something here, something a little more *momentous.*"

He called during the weekend, and I had until Monday morning to come up with something we could both live with, write it and Federal Express the results.

He urged me to make the trip for opening night, and I did. How many opening nights was I likely to see in a lifetime? I got into town early (too early), checked into a bed and breakfast and drank a bottle of wine waiting for show time. I only wish I hadn't been inexplicably sober when the house lights dimmed.

Unknown to me, the director had decided "Frank" should be played drunk. In the worst of ironies, I'd slugged down the stuff but it was my character who mimed the alcoholic haze. I'd heard tales of playwrights leaping onstage and going for the throats of actors who mauled their intentions, but my reaction, tellingly, was far less dramatic. When the slurring, stumbling Frankenstein I'd created entered stage left, my teeth began to chatter.

I didn't expect the actors and actresses to reincarnate the visual images in my head, but the extent of the divergence did startle me. Six of the seven were a good twenty years older than written, which put a crimp in the cut-throat careerism theme. Once I gave up on the visuals, I closed my eyes, trying to hear whether the dialogue sounded natural or like some bad translation of an alien code. When the surrounding audience started to giggle—not at the drunk or at anything I'd meant to sound funny—I covered my ears as well.

Every problem inherent in my botched short story resurfaced, this time live, onstage and magnified. I sincerely wished my diners would ditch the script and run screaming down the aisles like the Charenton insane. I thought about running screaming for the exit myself, but that would have required a performance of my own, exposure of another sort, and a species of bravery I couldn't muster at that particular moment. I stayed until the end, made myself stay, then stumbled out to the street in a trance that rivaled any sleepwalker's, wondering whatever possessed me to attempt to write for the stage.

But even then, a fresh failure, I knew the reason. Experiment, deviate, we learned at Governor's School. Loyal alumnae feel compelled to stick their necks out every now and again and risk a risk—just to prove we remember the motto.

Instruction

The semester I was hired to teach composition at a university whose administration imagined the institution up and coming in the small, liberal arts category, I was one of seventeen adjunct instructors in an English Department with a core faculty of ten. Before the semester officially began, my colleagues and I attended several meetings that emphasized the department's commitment to fine writing and the writing program. We were encouraged to adhere to the policy that forbade a D student from progressing to the next course level—to "grade tough."

The chairman offered me an additional one-hour weekly workshop in which I might, "for example," lecture on Sylvia Plath's "Ariel," discuss the finished poem, examine its many revisions and evaluate the effectiveness of each.

Sixteen researched, composed and delivered hour-long lectures for one third of thirteen hundred dollars.

I declined.

Yet mine wasn't a typical response. The vast majority of the adjunct staff were dedicated teachers who labored at that miserable pay scale for four, five, even seven consecutive years, moonlighting to pay the rent. Full-time appointments consistently went to outsiders to enhance the department's regional reputation. Adjuncts tended to remain adjuncts. During my one semester, a delegation launched a protest and met with the dean. He lamented conditions, called the problems of adjunct life "very grave indeed," but claimed his hands were tied. The university didn't have the money to increase adjunct wages, he said within throwing distance of a brand new, multi-million-dollar gym.

Although by and large we remained a nameless, faceless mass to the administration, within the department I gained fleeting recognition for reneging on spring semester commitments two weeks into the fall term. I apologized in writing to the chairman, but I could make more money in fewer hours waitressing. For a week or so fellow instructors stopped me in the hall with variations of "I hear you'd rather be a waitress." I adjusted my reply to match their supportive or sarcastic tones, but, either way, once I announced my intention to bolt, no one went out of his or her way to bond.

Office space for both instructors and professors in the humanities was severely limited. My assigned office was partitioned off into three sections. Four of us from the English Department used the third desk in shifts. In the cubicle ahead of ours, Tom, a professor of philosophy, tried to streamline logic for students who insisted they had to *know exactly* what a rule meant before they could plug it into an equation. ("That's just the way my mind *works!*")

I liked Tom; he was a wry, generous man, but listening to that daily tug of war exhausted me. No doubt my student conferences exhausted him. Jammed together without soundproofing, we heard every frustrated, weary sigh by default.

A Chinese professor occupied the cubicle ahead of Tom's, the one nearest the door. A tiny woman, she kept her chair snug against the far wall, the only one of our group who seemed to have more space than she cared to occupy. When two of us from English goofed and scheduled simultaneous conferences, she generously gave up her own desk, taking her lunch break at 10 A.M. As much as I appreciated the sacrifice, there was something utterly deflating about teachers rushing about, dislodging other teachers from their work spaces, squeezing in here and there, dragging a line of bewildered students behind them.

In composition courses, departmental policy required at least one teacher-student conference per student per semester to discuss ongoing papers, revisions, difficulties, gripes. I met with Carmen between papers one and two. She trembled in my presence and seemed eager to please the teacher if only she could discover how. Her proposed topic of "a trip somewhere north—I think we went to Connecticut" didn't do the trick. Together we tried to brainstorm an alternative.

She went blank-eyed.

What about childhood? Secret haunts? Favorite aunt? Hated cousin? A scary incident? A happy one?

"We did live in a bad neighborhood in Johnson City," she whispered faintly.

After an hour of probing, I thought we'd dredged up enough material to fill eight typed pages and probably thirty.

Every day she lived in Johnson City she cried. Teenage gangs terrorized her block. Burglars broke into her house while she hid under a bed. Her brother's drugged-out buddy, like some specter, knocked on their door by the hour, continuing to knock even after someone agreed to let him in. Her mother carried a gun.

Her dog was shot, her cat run over.

Did Carmen think she could write about that experience?

She meekly nodded.

"Yes ma'am, I think so."

Had I been able to score the telling, she would have fared better, grade-wise. Her deadpan tone worked well against the dog and cat carcasses, the gutted cars, her adventures in living at the tender age of five. Then or soon after, Carmen must have tagged the world a mean, irrational place because she sat before me a heart-breakingly resigned eighteen.

After our session, I canceled the rest of my conferences for the day, drove home, climbed into bed and slept the dead sleep of the depressed for fifteen hours straight.

Classes canceled less easily. Monday, Wednesday and Friday, twenty-two students at ten o'clock and twenty-four at noon awaited my instruction. I talked and questioned, they occasionally answered, yawned, stared and doodled in their notebooks. I began to dream of students piling into my house, crowding my typewriter, insinuating themselves around the legs of my desk.

Brad, a Navy man, had already published a story, as he constantly pointed out. He already *knew* how to write, and not the choppy sentences I liked either. Sentences that flowed.

"What makes you think I prefer choppy sentences?" I asked.

"The paragraph you picked to read aloud in class . . . *choppy!*" he fumed. "I can tell you aren't going to understand a *thing* I write."

Laura was Brad's character foil—trusting, earnest, a front-row sitter, the kind of student who makes a teacher hesitate to issue all those thundering composition commands: Active not passive voice! Show, don't tell! She took my every word as law, and she treated all laws with far too much reverence.

I noticed her Monday absence because, until that day, she hadn't missed a single class. Just before the bell, she knocked on the door, then stepped back into the hallway.

"I can't stay," she said when I joined her.

She didn't need to say anything else. I'd seen that expression before.

With students invading my dreams, once off-campus I strove to keep my distance, but I gave Laura my home phone number. In the weeks that followed we sometimes met at the local Pizza Hut where I drank coffee and she drank nothing, ate nothing.

"His eyes were so . . ." she began, never fully able to describe the terribleness of his eyes.

She remembered hearing her dress tear, the feeling that what was happening couldn't be happening to her. She might have been talking to any woman, but she talked to me, her English teacher. I listened as I have listened to other horrid, enraging accounts of women being raped in their homes, in their beds, with their children watching; women going about their business, going about their lives and then one morning, one afternoon, one black night, being taken cruelly by surprise. In Laura's case it happened on a date, her first in five years. The man was a friend of a friend. They'd met and talked over coffee and donuts. She liked him, trusted her instincts about liking him—instincts she'd probably never trust again.

She'd spoken with the staff of the Rape Crisis Center, the police, her school advisor, the Dean of Student Affairs and assorted others. She didn't need to hear another opinion and I didn't give it. The decision to prosecute or not rested with her, whatever I thought. But as we sat at that fake wood table in the red-curtained

Pizza Hut, I could feel her disappointment with my silence. I was her teacher. Teachers were supposed to tell people what to do.

As the semester wore on and I read more and more pages describing girlfriend/boyfriend troubles, accounts of first drunks, testimonials to Jesus, evaluations of cafeteria food, of on-campus parking, of registration procedures, what all forty-six wanted to be and do when they grew up, I began to feel as if I, personally, toted the collective weight of all those experiences and expectations. However poorly or wonderfully that information had been conveyed, I became its repository, data banking the intimacies of forty-six lives. I began to feel as if I should be responding to the issues that drove the prose: abuse, depression, grief—although I wasn't remotely qualified to undertake that counseling role. Eventually I began to wonder what qualified me or gave me the right to red-mark their sentences. In a dangerous slide from the educator's viewpoint, I couldn't believe the niceties of style took precedence over the purge of rawer communication.

Mark enrolled late in my class. Computer error. Consequently I didn't receive his one-page "Life So Far" summary until the end of the semester.

My full name is, he wrote. *I was born on my oldest brother's birthday. It was my brother that named me.*

I come from an unusual family. My siblings and I grew up in a "hell raising" atmosphere. My mother and father came from illiterate families. It was not unusual for our "father" (again, his quotes) *to get drunk and slap Mom around and target shoot inside the house with a pistol. Luckily my dad died when I was small. My family and I came to North Carolina from Illinois. It was tuff but everyone made it ok. My brothers and sisters moved out and started their own life when I was about nine or ten. Things were cool until my mom remarried. We moved several times about the country. Moving to a new place was frightening, but the worst part about it was dealing with my stepfather. He drank a lot. He was a small man with an oversize mouth. I use to listen to him for hours talk down on everyone under the sun. He would put down my mother, myself and especially my brother. I hated hearing that about my brother and there was nothing I could do about it. I never understood what my mother saw in that bum, but love is strange. After listening to him I would get so sad and depressed I would slip off to make collect calls to my brother. He wanted to help me so bad but there was nothing he could do. The conversations would always make me cry. One day my mom and stepfather were going to South Carolina to visit relatives. They were going on a weekday and I was told they would be back before I got home from school. Well I beat them home by a great deal. I stayed at the house for about two weeks wondering about them. I didn't call the police or nothing because I suspected something in the first place. I finally called my brother and I've lived a somewhat normal life ever since.*

It wasn't my job to discuss good or bad times with Mark, to congratulate him on his fortitude or wish him a less disrupted future. I'd been hired to correct his comma splices, his dangling modifiers, his run-on sentences. But after reading *Luckily my dad died when I was small,* I set aside my pen.

Almost Alone
in Albuquerque

Without intending to meet Carmelita, I did, in Albuquerque, when I rented a room in the northwest sector of that city. Every window was bolted shut for reasons of air conditioning, and all windows except one were shaded by a porch. The exception might have brightened the place considerably, but the enormous dresser shoved flat against it blocked all but the thinnest edge of morning light. Morning and afternoon, I tried to shove and shoulder that obstruction aside without success. For all my huffing and puffing, the dresser never moved more than a few centimeters in any direction.

Six days out of seven, Carmelita taught others how to wash, dry and clip miniature and standard poodles, schnauzers, cockapoos and any other pure or mixed breed that came through the doors of the Tara Lara School of Dog Grooming. She was a fast groomer, a good instructor, and while she worked she wore a blue smock over her blouse and a red scarf over her richly black knee-length hair. In twenty-five years she'd only cut it twice. The first time, her father cried. She said she inherited her father's Indian features and her mother's Spanish moods, as black as the hair on her head.

Factually, without the slightest hint of emotion, Carmelita discussed her abbreviated childhood, meals of dog and rattlesnake on the reservation, her move south. The black moods were but one hardship on a very long list. Regarding hardship, however, Carmelita's attitude was staunchly deterministic. She believed absolutely in fate and, because she did, she had no use for analysis or sympathy.

Her ex-husband Frankie counted as a hardship not because she regretted their marriage but because he was someone she still loved despite their divorce. Twice she mentioned the possibility of a reunion: once, rather wistfully; again, as if voicing the inevitable. Occasionally he drove down from South Dakota to visit, and they spent the weekend together in Carmelita's apartment decorated with standard-brand furniture and two crossed eagle feathers. He didn't care for Albuquerque, and she hated the reservation. For the time being, he wouldn't stay with her and she wouldn't return with him.

Frankie was a name I first heard the day she found me frantically cleaning my dim, rented room. Observing from the doorway, she mentioned that she'd cleaned twice a day, every day, before she left him.

"Before I left Frankie and before I had the breakdown," she said.

I stopped dusting, waiting for more if she cared to express it, but she let that pause spread to every corner and settle without speaking. In my presence she never used the word "breakdown" again.

In Frankie's absence, an orphan who called her Aunt Toni sporadically spent the night, but usually Carmelita lived alone with her tabby, Patches. She was extremely attached to the cat. When it wandered onto the highway and got hit by a car, a neighbor called the grooming salon. She accompanied Carmelita to the vet's office and heard the doctor announce he could save the life but not the limb. It was the owner's decision to euthanize, the neighbor said; it was Carmelita who didn't believe in saving crippled animals, not even ones she loved. When I visited that afternoon, the cat food, kitty litter and toys had already vanished.

The same week I stopped by to offer condolences she wouldn't accept, I also visited a fortune teller on the outskirts of Old Town, the city's prime tourist draw. By and large Sister Kay and her establishment supplied what the tourists demanded: bangles, beads, scarves and incense. Among those candles and ceramic saints, I laid bare my palm. Sister Kay didn't touch the flesh or long ponder its message. So-called friends wished me harm. A late-summer journey would alter my life. A dark halo surrounded and threatened my entire being. To erase it, I'd have to provide a new washcloth, a clean glass, a jar of distilled water and a minimum of $150 in cold cash—$300 if I wanted to obliterate the curse forever.

I thought the escapade would amuse Carmelita, unaware that she was deeply superstitious about fortune tellers, palm readers or any who trafficked in prophecies. Throughout my telling she sat stone-faced beneath her eagle feathers.

"You were wrong to go," she said when I finished.

A lark, I explained, a joke—but I'd inadvertently trampled another tenet of her code and she refused to see the humor.

"You never should have gone," she said and kept saying with spooky, unnerving certainty.

I should have met Judy before Carmelita. Judy not only appreciated the adventure of Sister Kay in story form, after hearing it, she trooped off for a read-out of her own hand map.

Judy, too, had recently arrived in the city. We introduced our-selves passing over the glinting wreckage of a TWA jet, travelling to the summit of the Sandia Mountains on the longest distance of unsupported cable in the world, according to the tramway's bro-chure. She and her Labrador Nicker had made the trip from Alaska to Albuquerque in an unheated Triumph in five days. Wowed by that achievement, I congratulated her. She seemed confused by the compliment. Later I understood why. If Sister Kay had warned Judy of dark and hovering haloes, she would have shaken them off through sheer accelerating speed.

Previous to Alaska, she'd tried Montana and horse breeding, Korea and teaching. In Alaska she drove a bus of pipeliners to and from their work sites, earning "terrific money" she then invested in Alaskan real estate. In Albuquerque she was vaguely consider-ing marriage to "this guy (she) knew," although she wasn't wild about committing herself "that far in advance."

Increasingly bored in Albuquerque, she offered me her twenty-four-hour chauffeuring services to the Foodway, to pool halls, shopping malls, anywhere I needed or wanted to go. When she heard I'd been in residence almost a month without touring Santa Fe, we headed north, Nicker wedged between us. Along the way, near a disappointingly narrow band of the Rio Grande, we stopped for a drive-in lunch. Predictably, the tacos and enchiladas were too hot for my palate, too bland for Judy's. She with her Nordic and I with my Cracker markings stood out among the noon-time crowd until the passengers of a silver van made the lot of us seem ordinary. Two bald men and a single bald woman dressed in flowing white and armed with bowie knives waited bare-foot on the scorching pavement for their own taco platters.

The bowie knives strapped to their waists impressed even Judy. When the van left, we tailgated, Nicker yelping as the Triumph skidded dangerously on mountain switchbacks. I had a lap full of guacamole, but that was the least of my worries. Judy didn't seem to compute the dangers of provoked paranoia; she was having fun. But as soon as she wasn't, as soon as the excitement cooled and the chase grew stale, she banked into a u-turn and we headed back.

For the brief time I could, I ran with Judy, propelled by her energy. Then one morning I found her adios note taped to my door. At some late hour of the previous night, she'd decided to pay her sister in Alabama a visit.

Sorry not to say goodbye in person, she wrote, but she couldn't bear to wait until morning, to waste all that potential road time.

I understood.

Given the opportunity, Judy would always drive through darkness into light. She was lucky that way. The preference came naturally.

At the summit of the Sandia Mountains, from the lookout post next to the cable cars, the city appeared to be a checkerboard of darkness and light, a plain composed of symmetrical squares: these in brightness, those in shadow. The emptiness and clarity of the desert seemed vastly superior to my humid, overgrown homeland: a climatic and visual relief. Gazing at Albuquerque from that height, I wanted to see a new landscape and tried, but what I really saw was how that ground diverged from my primary base.

Humans like to think they can get away by getting away, but troubles travel.

I only had a few weeks left in Albuquerque when I met a woman who didn't have the funds or the leisure for moping in the abstract. She was pregnant with her second child in as many years, and her husband, Jeff, was unemployed. He'd managed a fast food restaurant before an automobile accident mangled his spine and made prolonged standing impossible. They were a couple who seemed to be perpetually waiting for the insurance settlement that would lift them out of their financial abyss, money sure to come next month or the month thereafter.

I approached Lila cautiously and with a great deal of apprehension. She reminded me of girls I'd feared on the playground, tough to the bone. We didn't become friends; we barely became acquaintances. Nonetheless, certain ground rules applied. I didn't see Jeff without Lila, and when I did see him, I didn't talk with him in any prolonged, animated way. The Jeff restrictions weren't devised especially for me. They applied to any female, married or single. Since Lila's husband didn't interest me in the least, I had no problem avoiding those hot spots of jealousy and possession, but in other areas compliance and silence were more difficult to sustain.

To share Lila's company, one had to refrain from debating her prejudices. She disliked, generically and individually, Indians, Mexicans and the "coyote" mix. Her sense of justice stopped abruptly at the borders of me and mine, and she lashed out at anything or anyone she perceived as a threat to her family's dwindling rights.

I didn't join her closed circle; I didn't really try, knowing that when I left Albuquerque—no longer available for ice cream and late night pizza, no longer a tagalong to Jeff's parents' home where the fourteen-year-old brother drank his vodka straight, where the unwed sister bragged that her baby's paternal grandfather rated as the city's wealthiest contractor, where dogs, cats, babies and adults snarled and charged each other as a matter of course—when I dropped from sight, I'd also drop from mind as all people and events not inextricably bound to Lila's everyday always dropped. I also knew that the moment I disappeared I'd become just another enemy to despise and abuse: someone with a plane ticket, someone who could pick up and go. Regardless, I wanted to say goodbye and called from the airport.

When Jeff answered, I was surprised—Lila typically played censor. But she wasn't around to play censor that day; she'd been hospitalized with labor pains the night before. At such a premature stage of development, their baby was at risk, Jeff said, quoting the doctor. All in all the medical establishment wasn't offering much hope or encouragement. As usual for Jeff and Lila, the statistics went against them.

I dialed the number of her hospital room without planning exactly what I'd say when or if she answered. As her extension rang and rang, an old, irrational, childhood fear set in, insisting everyone I cared about was dying.

Lila will die, I thought. Her baby will die.

It was the fear of someone who had the luxury of treating presentiment as fact, who gave in to dread and premature defeat, and in Lila's case that reaction missed the mark. In Lila's case, I failed to factor in the enormous quantity of revenge that she satisfied, surviving in a world that expected less.

Both Lila and her baby survived. I, too, survived, jetting home over mountains strewn with the debris of pilot error, but the victory felt shaky, and for an unhealthy stretch of time I didn't consider the pilot's success my particular good fortune.

Death Valley Allure

On my first Death Valley adventure, I entered by way of Shoshone and Route 178. I didn't get far into the terrain—not even as far as Jubilee Pass, famous for its spring outburst of brilliantly colored wildflowers in a vista otherwise dominated by tufts of cattle spinach, desert holly and creosote bushes, vegetation that not only survives but thrives on a miserly 1.6 inches of rain per year. The constriction and brevity of that first trip in wasn't my choice or doing. My travelling companion wasn't enamored of deserts or Precambrian rock forms or sweeping gravel fans. His head wasn't turned nor his heart engaged by clarity of air, blueness of sky or the way heat shimmered like a mirage above the Valley floor. He didn't warm to the illusion of emptiness. Stillness made him uneasy. He loved cityscapes and the bustling crowds that inhabited them. When he looked out onto that unpeopled stretch of the Mojave, he was not pleased.

Only I was pleased, enchanted actually, by the vista and its beginning-of-time feel. Within that billion-year configuration of sun, sky and land, human beings represented the off-note, the superfluous element. Not one of those 3,200 square miles of dolomite, quartzite, shale and limestone needed you; the sky didn't need you; the sun didn't need you. At best you were an afterthought, a momentary interloper; at worst a despoiling polluter. While my companion stayed put in our air-conditioned rental car, I ventured out alone into that glittery, desolate landscape and promptly fell in love.

Once upon a time Death Valley glittered with gold. An argonaut named Rowan and two Mormon missionaries discovered the Valley's first gold nugget December 1, 1849. Thereafter, inflamed by the possibilities, fortune seekers piled in from near and far, creating a region littered with pocket miners by the late nineteenth century. A second brief gold boom occurred in the 1890s, enriching the nearby town of Rhyolite, but the greatest riches Death Valley had to offer came in the form of salts, especially borax. William Tell Coleman tapped that profit vein with the founding of the Harmony Borax Company. Television made famous the twenty-mule teams that hauled the four-ton wagons out of the Valley; less famous were the Chinese laborers who mined the borax for $1.50 a day and made Mr. Coleman a wealthy man.

Before the 49ers, horse traders crossed the 45 waterless, blistering miles between Bitter Springs and Salt Springs on the journey from New Mexico to California, a route they called "jornada del muerto." Before the horse traders, Death Valley belonged to the Shoshone, Paiute and Kawaiisu tribes. And before that, way before, scientists speculate, the land belonged to water birds, camels, mastodons and saber-toothed tigers. A fresh water lake, 600 feet deep, created from the spillover of Sierra Nevada glaciers, nourished those beasts. What's left of the lake at the end of the twentieth century is Salt Creek, home of the pupfish, a tiny, two-mile creek as briny as the ocean, a trickle in an otherwise dry and dusty desert.

Naturalists, park rangers, even politicians who attempt to explain the allure of Death Valley somehow feel they've short-changed their subject, left something out, miscommunicated the essence. In author Richard Lingenfelter's opinion, that inexplicable and unknowable element accounts for much of the charm. "What sets (Death Valley) apart more than anything else is the mind's eye," he wrote in *Death Valley and the Amargosa: A Land of Illusion.* "(I)t is . . . a place in the mind, a shimmering mirage of riches and mystery and death."

Embattled prospectors who departed by way of the Panamint Mountains in 1850 supposedly coined the name "Death Valley." They left a smaller group than they arrived, having buried Richard Culverwell, the Valley's first recorded victim, in the flats. Weary and gold-less, at the top of the ridge they looked back just long enough to bid the graveyard adieu.

Despite its grisly title, in the almost 150 years since Culverwell's demise, fewer than 100 people have died in Death Valley. Two-thirds of that number expired from dehydration. Within its boundaries, on a hot summer day, humans can drop as much as two gallons of water doing nothing more strenuous than lounging in the shade. When the water loss reaches the three-gallon mark, bodily collapse is already underway. The tongue shrivels, the eyes sink; hearing becomes impaired. Flesh becomes striated with bloody cracks that parody the faulted Panamint and Amargosa mountains to the west and east. Should you die alone, the sun and heat and scavengers quickly reduce your unburied corpse to a heap of bleached bones. Ultimately what's left will color-coordinate with glistening calcium carbonate.

Perhaps the Valley's hazards heighten its allure. Perhaps danger is the allure, pure and simple. Packed with warnings and admonitions, park brochures emphasize the gravity of the risks: explosives in mine areas; flash flooding once those 1.6 inches of rain do fall; roaming packs of feral, biting animals.

Visitors, beware.

"Death Valley contains hundreds of abandoned mines and associated structures that are potentially dangerous. For your safety, use extreme caution in driving or walking around in the vicinity of all mine workings. Watch for open shafts, prospect holes and adits. Supervise children closely and never enter abandoned mines. STAY OUT AND STAY ALIVE.

"Be alert for flash floods when it looks stormy. Do not ford low places when water is running. Flood waters can undercut pavement or sweep a car from the road.

"All animals in the park are wild. They often carry diseases. Do not feed or disturb them."

The one-time turf of camels and mastodons is currently populated by coyotes, sidewinders, ravens, rabbits, deer, mountain lions, bobcats, bighorn sheep, foxes and burros. The burros are transplants, descendants of the pack animals brought in by the prospectors. Highly adaptive, they are proliferating at a rate that alarms park officials who place them high on the nuisance scale. At night they bray their way through campgrounds, drowning out the yipping coyotes. Most of the wildlife, burros included, do their roaming at night, smart enough to escape the blistering heat of the day.

Once a weather station was installed at Furnace Creek and temperatures in the Valley began to be systematically recorded, the area gained fame not only as the hottest spot in the country, but the hottest spot on earth with a July 1913 reading of 134 degrees Fahrenheit.

For six months, a park brochure informs the uninformed, "unmerciful heat dominates the scene." And for the remaining six months of the calendar year, that heat "releases its grip only slightly." Furthermore: "If your car develops vapor lock, wrap a wet rag around the fuel pump to speed cooling. If your car breaks down, stay with it. This is a harsh environment in the summer, and any emergency situation can easily become life-threatening."

And yet, 900 varieties of plants flourish in those severe conditions, some with roots that extend 10 times the height of the average tourist. The tourist industry is also flourishing. Attracted by the history, myths, reality and surreality of the place, millions visit annually and have since the turn of the century, when an enterprising sort built a toll road at Stove Pipe Wells. Even Hollywood came calling. In the 1920s Director Eric von Stroheim shot the final scenes of *Greed* in the heart of the Valley.

Two tourists who extended their stay were Albert and Bessie Johnson, owners of Death Valley Ranch, the many roomed, many towered "castle," built in the 1920s, that required its own water supply, sewer, ice plant, and hydroelectric generator. The Johnsons furnished their vacation home with Minorcan rugs, hand-tooled leather drapes, a $125,000 organ and Walter Scott, a cowboy prospector and one-time member of Buffalo Bill Cody's "Wild West" show. The wait to tour the Johnson extravaganza, advertised as "Scotty's Castle," can stretch to three hours in the summer months, but visitors can avoid that aberration and tour instead the real marvels of the park: Ubehebe Crater, 2,400 feet across and 1,000 years young, the glories of Golden Canyon, the curves and coveys of the sand dunes near Stovepipe Wells, and Badwater, lowest point on the Western Hemisphere, dipping 282 feet below sea level. For all the off-roadsters and RVs and 49er festivals and film crews, determined folk can still find a spot of absolute solitude, a place to sit and think and *hear* Death Valley's very distinctive brand of silence. People have described that quiet as "deep," "primordial," "inspirational" and "restorative." It leaves its mark. For a while, after one hears it, modern life sounds like a shriek.

These days I enter Death Valley from the west and Route 190, descending from the Panamints past the Emigrant campsite and down another eight miles into the village of Stovepipe Wells. For sheer spectacle nothing comes close to that wide-angled view, especially near the end of the day as the light shifts and ricochets off the mountains, streaking, then withdrawing, from the desert below.

It took me fifteen years to get back to Death Valley after my too-brief introduction, and by now I've returned often enough for the negatives associated with the first sighting to have eroded a bit and loosened their grip—or so one would think. When I arrive, while I'm in residence, I'm spared the recollection. It only resurfaces as I pack to leave, regretful of my imminent departure. Then I remember the negotiations, trade-offs and sworn promises associated with my first drop-in. I remember the revving Chevrolet engine, the impatient driver at the wheel. I remember the window rolling down a hairsbreadth and the shouts that echoed: enough, let's go, get in. And I remember myself turning from vast, open space to climb into a closed box of recycled air and resume an argument that continued back to Los Angeles, back to the South and back to a kudzu-smothered farmhouse.

"Never travel alone," a park brochure warns. "Always tell someone where you are going and when you expect to return."

Maybe so, but I should have taken my chances anyway—waved off my companion, started walking and kept walking, because there are worse things to become than bleached bones. Resigned and hopeless, to name two.

Testing

Take the sour
if you take me
         W. B. Yeats, *"Crazy Jane on the Day of Judgment"*

Once I believed I wanted to become a clinical psychologist. I liked psychology courses, particularly the freshman course that required a paper on "personal conditioning." For that assignment, we investigated our childhoods and tracked the environmental variables. Although purely speculative conclusions were allowed, I opted for a pseudo-scientific approach. I sent out a sheaf of questionnaires with a cover letter that claimed the "university" survey was anonymous and the responses to it strictly confidential. Three lies, altogether. Then I devised a stapling code—one staple, two staples, three; one slanted, two slanted, two crossed—and noted the pattern beside each name on my list. Basically I was looking to tag sexist trends.

I mailed copies to my parents, my brother, my first grade teacher, the preacher at Providence Baptist Church, my original high school basketball coach and sundry others. The preacher signed his name on the last page in a show of nothing-to-hide pride. My basketball coach drove to another town to mail his reply, ensuring a different postmark. (Cagey, but not quite cagey enough.) Without exception everyone replied and replied speedily.

Mrs. Brumsey had taught my entire family first grade—father, mother, brother, me. At the time of my mailing, she must have been seventy but her attitudes were far from old-fashioned. On questions one through twenty-five she consistently argued for the equal treatment of the sexes. Such consistency made me remember the time she torpedoed a feminine wiles scheme of mine. When my best friend Rhonda stole my second-grade boyfriend Glenn, to get even, I spread the rumor that he'd kissed me at recess. Someone told Mrs. Brumsey, who collected Glenn from his class, then called me to the front of ours.

"*Did* you kiss her?"

"No ma'am, no ma'am," he stuttered, rightly terrified.

I did what I could to save face: turned haughty, turned on my heel, turned away from both of them to announce to the class at large that maybe Glenn hadn't been the mysterious kisser, but *someone* had sneaked up on the playground and planted a smoocheroo.

Mrs. Brumsey left it at that. Perhaps she realized that the more cornered I felt, the more flagrantly I'd lie. Or maybe she wrote me off then and there as a hard core fibber. A fairly accurate assessment, if so. Twelve years later I was still giving her the runaround.

I enjoyed the lecture courses in experimental, abnormal and developmental psychology, but the practicum experience unnerved me. Undergraduate majors had to choose two "therapeutic settings" for volunteer work. After much dithering I settled on John Umstead Hospital in Butner and the recreational therapy department of UNC-Memorial.

It took almost an hour by car to reach John Umstead, and

those of us who spent part of the fall semester in residence always seemed to arrive on the grayest day of the week. We travelled as a motorcade, three carloads of aspiring healers in jeans and granny glasses, determined to ignore the stench of urine, vomit and sweat no disinfectant, no matter how strong, could mask. My in-house assignment was the geriatric ward. Volunteers were matched with specific patients and each week we were supposed to visit him or her, sit alongside, converse and listen, if ever he or she spoke. We also kept bingo markers on the appropriate squares.

Many students spent time there as time was meant to be spent, attempting to establish contact through the various drug layers, to jar memories and stave off further retreats into catatonia and despair. I didn't do nearly so well. Distracted by the pea green walls, the blurry television set, the dozens of down-in-the-heel bedroom slippers, the mutterers, the dazed rockers, the fearful window huggers, I couldn't concentrate on my single charge. I kept contemplating the space between me and them, the space between them and them, the space between mind and body. All too frequently the gap was overwhelming and unbridgeable, a free-float of isolation.

After a few trips to Butner, I looked forward to working with children in a gym. I imagined the experience would be less distressing to the outsider. It *was* more active (for volunteers and patients). But most of that activity came off fitful, frantic and not altogether healthy. One little boy loved to sing "Jeremiah was a bullfrog"—just that snatch of lyric. As he sang it, he spun and twirled, his voice climbing the register, his feet dancing faster and faster, stimulation begetting stimulation, until one of the trained staff intervened and carted him, kicking and screaming, back to his room.

Theoretically, if I entered private practice and catered specifically to neurotic suburbanites, I could avoid such scenes. But could I persuade anyone, even the minorly stressed, to believe in change, progress, bright lights at the end of dark tunnels? It seemed unlikely. So I did potential clients, the American Psychological Association and myself a favor and reneged on further training. The right decision, but at the time it left me career-less.

To rectify that lack, I signed up for the Kuder Occupational Interest Survey and the Strong-Campbell Interest Inventory tests at the university counseling center. For fifty dollars, my interests and proclivities were profiled and cross-matched and the results discussed with me by a job counselor.

"Fascinating," mine said, probably always said, to encourage the person sitting across from him, rigid with suspense. "You have most in common with a lighthouse keeper."

I gawked.

"Aren't lighthouses automated these days?"

"Try to relax," he said.

My second aggregate suggested a career in entertainment. Did I, by chance, sing? (Somewhere besides in the shower, the car or at 4-H Club talent shows, he meant.)

We moved on. The similarities construct a bust, he tried the opposite tack. I had least in common with x-ray technicians, life insurance agents and directors of Christian education programs.

After giving up on academic solutions, I sought wiggier sources of advice and classification. A handwriting analysis revealed that my "difficulties" stemmed from "important events in my childhood." (Always a safe bet.) My personality "tended to be intense" and "somewhat aggressive." Very often I "preferred to keep others at arm's length"—others who, "in general," found me "difficult to understand."

A clash between my Taurus sun and Gemini moon accounted for my "perennial psychic struggle," according to the American Astrological Association. "Essentially yours is going to be a life of work," my printout predicted. "There is a tendency to be appointed to secretarial positions. Because Mercury is your ruler, Death constitutes permanent preoccupation. You will be plagued throughout life with nervous stress. In your middle years you will express yourself in a very strange manner. Take time for introspection," the horoscope concluded. "You have a great need to eliminate many of the undesirable memories of your subconscious."

Me, and the rest of the world.

In homage to my one-time career choice, I took one last "defining" test, the Rorschach. As required, I didn't know the technician. A psychologist-friend arranged for her help on the sly. In answering, I was supposed to describe not only the images the inkblots suggested but also an explanation of why they appeared so.

For the first few cards I chattered on: two witches on a motorcycle, a cat mask with horns.

"Halloween as a theme," I said.

"Anything else?" the technician asked.

Something about her tone made me scale back the balance of my answers. But I could have gone on at great length—bats in flight, fringed leather vests, women gossiping, polar bears scaling tundra, the game of pattycake. And all that *before* turning the cards upside down.

Once my responses had been entered into the computer and tabulated, my psychologist-friend invited me to lunch at Highland

Hospital and handed over the results. I might as well have stayed with the horoscope's evaluation. The Rorschach echoed my negativity ("a much more negative person than most"). I "tended to interpret situations in an overly personalized manner, set goals beyond my functioning capacities." I existed in "a chronic state of tension." I was a "guarded, distant, pessimistic" sort.

The difference lay in the labeling. According to the Rorschach, my cluster of traits fell in the psychotic zone.

"This subject suffers severe ideational slippage," the summation read. "These test results indicate the very distinct possibility of schizophrenia."

"All writers are schizophrenic," another friend dismissed. "Something to do with seeing words as more than words. You know, the reverberations."

Unfortunately I heard that comforting theory much later, long after I'd received my disturbing profile and ventured from Highland's cafeteria to visit the site of Zelda Sayre Fitzgerald's fiery demise. Zelda, writer, wife of a more famous writer. Zelda, diagnosed schizophrenic.

Because no family member of mine had arranged for the Rorschach or had me committed to a psychiatric facility while awaiting its verdict, I could stand quietly and pay my respects for as long as I liked. And when I had finished my tribute, I could tuck my damning scores under my arm, head for my car, leave the grounds and no orderly would give chase. Unlike sedated Zelda, confined in her fifth floor lock-up behind chained windows, I remained at liberty. But the longer I stood over her charred bones on the grounds of Highland Hospital, the more imperiled that liberty seemed, so I turned and ran like hell.

The
Confessions
of Willie Mae Hall

Highland Hospital, the oldest psychiatric facility in the Southeast, is a private institution with a reputation for treating difficult,
end of the road cases. Originally called Dr. Carroll's Sanitarium
in honor of its founder, Robert Carroll, it opened in downtown
Asheville, North Carolina in 1904 with a roster of eleven patients,
several of whom were wealthy enough to accompany the doctor
and his wife on trips around the world. In 1909 the enterprise
moved to its current location, a prettier, nine-acre spread on
Zillicoa Street. The Carroll cure stressed the importance of climate, diet and exercise in regaining mental equilibrium. In the
early days, Highland patients ate vegetarian, avoided tobacco,
drugs and alcohol, and took part in a daily program of calis-
thenics, volleyball and gardening. These days cafeteria chow
includes several kinds of meat as well as rich desserts, sports
are not a requirement, and professional gardeners tend the lawns.
Although it remains an expensive hospital ($2,000+ per week
for room and board, doctors' fees and medication charged

separately), the majority of patients, less than rich, rely on medical insurance to pay the tab.

The majority of those still intrigued by the 1948 Highland Hospital fire are drawn by its most famous fatality: Zelda Fitzgerald, burned down to her shoes while locked on the fifth floor of Central Building where chains, not bars, kept the windows from opening wide enough for a body to escape institutionalization or death. Forty years after the event, Highland continues to field requests regarding Zelda's schizophrenia, her day-to-day delusions and hallucinations. But when I made the trip up Highland's curving, tree-lined driveway I was less interested in Zelda's psychiatric tear sheet than in one of her keepers: Willie Mae Hall, the supervisor on duty when smoke turned to fire in the vicinity of the dumb waiter shaft of Central's diet kitchen, March 10.

The official line is Zelda's records burned with Zelda, that, for the groupie as well as the scholar, there's simply nothing left to review. Highland administrators also refuse to discuss Willie Mae Hall. But with regard to Willie Mae, the information blackout poses less of an obstacle. Employer preference aside, in the wake of what the local press dubbed "the greatest tragedy in Buncombe County history," much of the night supervisor's life and deeds entered the public domain, available for public consumption. As her court-appointed psychiatrist testified, as the court heard and as the *Asheville Citizen-Times* reported, Willie Mae routinely carried a box of matches on her person when she made her rounds. Asked why, she explained that she often had trouble finding matches when she needed them.

The question is: did she need a match, did she use one, March 10 near midnight to ignite the diet kitchen? The woman herself believed so. Two weeks after the inquest, Willie Mae turned herself in to authorities, confessed to starting the blaze, and asked to be jailed. Allowed to remain free, she said, she feared she would commit other monstrous crimes.

Reporter J. Hart Snyder called the fire a "midnight holo-caust." His colleague, Al Erxleben, chose a more apocalyptic des-cription: "Death rode on the sound of low moans, whimpers and high-pitched screams as flames licked through the wooden timbers. . . . Screams echoed and echoed . . . above the sound of water being poured through rakish door frames and blackened, jagged window panes. . . ." (*AC-T* 3/11/48)

Nine women patients died. Central Building, containing sev-eral wards, a laboratory, food supplies and medical stock, was to-tally destroyed. Director Basil T. Bennett estimated that property and equipment damage exceeded $300,000. The town's fire chief clocked the first summons for help at 11:44 P.M., the second at 11:50 P.M. In his opinion, the fire burned forty to forty-five min-utes before that help arrived. Twenty-two patients were safely evacuated, but during the chaos many of them strayed off hospital grounds and into the nearby woods.

Newspaper accounts claimed "at least six registered nurses" were on duty the night of the fire, including Willie Mae Hall. The March 11 edition of the *Citizen-Times* quotes Willie Mae as saying no one was in the diet kitchen at the outbreak of the fire but that a coffee urn had been heating. She and the night watch-man were in Oak Lodge at the time, she volunteered, a structure that stood "a few yards to the rear of the destroyed building." (*AC-T* 3/12/48)

At the coroner's inquest, District Solicitor W. K. McLean rep-resented the state. Fifty-odd witnesses appeared before the court, among them the nurse in charge of Central Building, Doris Jane Anderson, who flew in to testify from Wisconsin where she'd been staying with her parents. (*AC-T* 3/27/48) A table three feet from the dumb waiter shaft was ablaze, she testified, but there was no coffee urn on it.

> "One bucket of water would have put out that fire, now wouldn't it?" Solicitor McLean asked.
> "Perhaps," Miss Anderson replied.
> "But you made no attempt to put it out, did you?"
> "No." (*AC-T* 3/27/48)

Rather than sling water, she tried to contact hospital authorities because 1) those were her orders; 2) she wasn't trained in firefighting "methods"; and 3) she'd never seen a "destroying" fire. It reminded her of "one of those fiery hoops animals jump through in circuses." (*AC-T* 3/27/48)

Her terror was given short shrift. Step by step, Solicitor McLean led her through her actions on the night of March 10. As part of her usual routine, she administered sedatives to Zelda and Zelda's fellow inmates. At 11:35 P.M. she entered the diet kitchen, saw the burning table, left the kitchen, returned, then left again for the fourth floor. From there she called Oak Lodge. In an emergency situation (she testified), she'd been instructed to summon help from Oak Lodge or Highland Hall. When she couldn't reach the hospital's private exchange, she tried the central exchange operator, but the Oak Lodge line was busy. Only then did she call the fire department.

That would indicate a lapse of almost ten minutes between the moment she sighted the fire and her reporting of it, the court noted, and the witness didn't challenge that conclusion.

Anderson's testimony followed the fire chief's and preceded Willie Mae Hall's. When Willie Mae took the stand, March 29, she swore Nurse Anderson had *not* been instructed to call Oak Lodge.

She also swore that when she completed her Central Building check at 11:20 P.M., no fire raged or smoldered. From Central she walked to Oak Lodge and remained there until she heard the fire truck sirens. (*AC-T* 3/29/48)

Whereas the solicitor took great pains to emphasize Doris Jane Anderson's ten-minute dereliction of duty, no court official questioned the half hour the supervisor remained in a building "a few yards to the rear" of the burning Central, unaware of the rampage. After she heard the sirens, she ran from Oak Lodge to take in the spectacle, she testified. She volunteered no circus metaphors à la her fellow employee. She didn't say (or the *Citizen-Times* didn't report) how long she watched the red and orange and yellow flames shoot from the roof of the doomed structure or how she felt about that brilliant inferno. No record of her response—horror or blatant fascination—exists.

Several Hall(s) appear on the noncomputerized, nonalphabetized list of 1948 defendants in the Buncombe County court archives before the April 13 notation regarding Willie Mae. On that date Judge J. Hoyle Sink "addressed the matter" of the Highland supervisor and ordered a psychiatric examination to be conducted by Dr. Wesley Taylor.

When court reconvened on April 14, Willie Mae's brother-in-law appeared to "offer such assistance or comfort as he might," the record stated.

> WILLIE MAE HALL: (Addressing the Court): "Do I have authority to forbid anybody to come in?"
> THE COURT: "Yes."
> WILLIE MAE HALL: "I don't want the children brought."
> THE COURT: "Yes, that is quite proper."

Which children? Her brother-in-law's? Anyone under the age of twelve? Regardless, the request was honored, and a recess called until the following morning. At that time Dr. Taylor delivered his verdict on the mental capacity of a forty-year-old, unmarried, certified nurse, born in Mississippi, raised in a Baptist orphanage, once knocked down by a train, once burned and scarred by a mangle, educated at The Woman's College of Hattiesburg, a fan of detective stories and the "occasional" romance.

After her nurse's training, for three years, Willie Mae worked at the Baptist Hospital in Jackson, Mississippi. She quit that first job (no cause given) to work as a private nurse "for a short time." Later, "for some time," she nursed at King's Daughter's Hospital in Brookhaven, leaving that post because of the low salary and because (she told Dr. Taylor) she didn't care for the work. (Nursing in general by then or the King's Daughter's set-up?)

From Brookhaven she moved on to a tubercular sanitarium in Sanitoria, Mississippi and stayed for ten years. In 1945 she returned "home to Pineola" where she bought a "small farm of fifty acres, with a fairly good house . . . occupied by a tenant farmer most of the time since."

Consider the range of possibilities that lurk between those clauses. *Finished with nursing/tired of administering to others/determined, for once, to please herself,* she returned home to Pineola. *Fulfilling a lifetime ambition/after inspecting one or ten or fifty farms,* she bought a plot that included *a two- or three-story house with adequate or caving chimneys.*

In one brief, summarizing sentence, Willie Mae Hall assumed land-owning and landlording duties, pulled up stakes, ran. When did the tenant farmer move in? What percentage of his crop paid the rent? Did she leave because she felt restless? Because of dwindling finances? Did farm life seem an idyll or a nightmare?

In any event, she took a job at the state mental hospital in

Jackson. Six months later, her doctor recommended a change of climate because of her severe asthma attacks, and she moved to Asheville. At Highland, she lived on the grounds in The Villa. She liked the residence, she told Dr. Taylor, because it was quiet and off duty she could sleep without being disturbed—could, that is, until Central caught fire and nine patients lost their lives.

"Since the fire, the sole subject of conversation in the hospital has been the fire," Dr. Taylor observed. "This has made a very great impression on a woman of Miss Hall's emotional temperament. She says she has dreamed of the fire practically every night since."

Arresting, persuasive dreams.

Via Dr. Taylor:

"In the first group she dream(ed) she saw and hear(d) a couple of patients, whom she knew quite well, calling and begging her to let them out of the building. . . . After a day or two the second form of dream crystallized. These same two patients complained to her that she had burned them up. . . . On Monday, April 12, she dreamt that these same two patients began to call to her, saying 'Since you burned us up, now go and burn Oak Lodge as well.'"

Only two of the nine haunted, but which two: Mrs. F. Scott Fitzgerald, Mrs. W. Bruce Kennedy, Mrs. Jules Doering, Mrs. G. C. Womack, Sarah Neely Hipps, Ida Engel, Janice Borochoff, Virginia Ward James, Marthina DeFriece? The two oldest? The two youngest? The shyest? The meanest?

As a result of the dreams (the doctor informed the court), Willie Mae Hall had not "slept well." With the exception of one night "almost immediately following the fire," she shunned the use of sedatives, preferring "to put up with her headaches and insomnia."

(And why wouldn't she shun sedation? Who at Highland,

sane or batty, swallowed a capsule without flashing on the nine once sedated, now fried?)

Dr. Taylor conceded that Willie Mae was "in the habit of passing through the kitchen numerous times every night." Indeed, he continued, "it would have been hard to explain why she had *not* (his emphasis) passed through shortly before (the fire)."

Although Dr. Taylor seemed at pains to clarify Willie Mae's presence in the kitchen, no one challenged her contradictory statements about when she became aware of the fire and where she was when she found out. Dr. Taylor's report said she "witnessed the fire almost from beginning to end." At the inquest, Willie Mae claimed the sirens alerted her—sirens on fire trucks that arrived, according to the fire chief, forty to forty-five minutes after ignition.

For the court's purposes, Dr. Taylor profiled Willie Mae Hall as a "quiet, reserved and sensitive woman," one who possessed a "vivid imagination" and a "keen conscience." She "tried to live up to the teachings of Christianity" which she believed were "right." He felt certain she had "(n)ever done anything in her life that she (was) ashamed to face."

At forty, she hadn't menstruated for six years. A nonsmoker, she had sampled alcohol "once or twice in her life." She carried "no grudges," didn't "hate people" or have "cause to (feel) revengeful." Before the onslaught of accusatory dreams, she didn't think about "burning buildings or setting fires." Although once, as a child, she had "set a curtain on fire . . . for the sake of seeing it burn." She also admitted involvement in several small blazes discovered in Central Building earlier that year, but Dr. Taylor dismissed the latter confession as hysteria, the first as unimportant, missing the symbolism entirely: as a little girl, Willie Mae Hall took a match to curtains in a Baptist orphanage, a place saturated with fire and brimstone rhetoric.

(Go to your room, Willie Mae. Stand in the corner, Willie Mae. Pray hard for your soul, Willie Mae. Your sins are black and heinous.)

The orphan who, unlike her colleague, had no Wisconsin family to fly home to once a pair of charred and vengeful ghosts began to haunt, couldn't explain to her doctor why she might *wish* to torch Central Building. She also couldn't "state positively that she did not light a match" to "deliberately . . . burn things up."

Subsequently she begged the court not to consult any Highland doctors about her case. If she "really did it," she said, she couldn't bear to face them or Director Bennett, whom she "like(d) and admire(d) very much." Nevertheless the director visited her in jail and suggested she needed treatment. Willie Mae readily agreed.

"An hysterical woman," Dr. Taylor concluded, "overworked and worried"; a person who placed "too much emphasis on dreams." He was willing to bet his reputation on the call that Willie Mae Hall had "nothing whatsoever to do with (the) fire.

"Cases like these are not uncommon by any means. It is well known that people connect themselves . . . with things which they have heard and which impress them emotionally. They admit to poisoning people they have never seen, or committing murders that did not occur. . . . It is one of the symptoms of hysteria. . . . If you ask me whether this woman is insane or not, I shall very definitely say that she is not. I believe she will recover. I know that she needs to get away. . . ."

On April 16, 1948 presiding Judge Sink agreed, remanding Willie Mae Hall to a distant "outstanding institution for observation and treatment."

An inconclusive finale.

I don't doubt that Willie Mae Hall came to question, in

Dr. Taylor's words, "everything of importance that might apply to her case," including her sanity. But I do have trouble dismissing out of hand the motive of vengeance.

Would a forty-year-old, asthmatic, menopausal, dream-driven, Baptist-reared orphan turned nurse trust a well-placed match to even the score? Rumors at Highland say yes.

An Emily/Sylvia Pilgrimage

On a rainy, windy, midweek day in September 145 years after Emily Brontë's death, her hometown in Yorkshire is thick with pilgrims. Funneled from parking lots built for chartered buses, directed by bilingual signs in English and Japanese, they climb up and down the steep, cobbled Main Street of Haworth, buying souvenirs, taking tea or downing a pint at the Black Bull, brother Branwell's favorite pub.

For the Brontë fan, there's quite a bit of territory to cover: the Parsonage Museum, administered by the Brontë Society since 1928; St. Michael's Church, where Patrick Brontë preached; the bleak graveyard between the church and parsonage and the moors beyond. The Haworth Information Center, stocked with maps, postcards, Brontë novels and biographies, is also hopping. Unrattled, its staff members patiently and thoroughly field questions, clearly the same questions they answer a hundred times a day.

At Hebden Bridge, the town below the tiny hill town of Heptonstall where Sylvia Plath's bones lie, the lone information clerk is equally patient but comparatively idle. She can direct me to Heptonstall's parish church but not precisely to Plath's grave. Given the legion of Plath fans, I'm surprised she can't. Then, again, only thirty years have passed since Sylvia's death. The tea shops and chartered bus tours may yet arrive.

I hadn't thought about Emily Jane Brontë and Sylvia Plath Hughes in tandem until visiting their graves in the space of a single afternoon. Authors born more than a century apart, they both died at thirty, literature's loss. One was the daughter of a nineteenth-century parson, the other the daughter of a twentieth-century educator expected to become a Lutheran minister by the grandparents who paid his college tuition. Both Emily and Sylvia were encouraged, even expected, to excel scholastically and artistically. They wrote, they sketched, they grew up taller than average—Emily leveling off at 5' 7", Sylvia at 5' 9". As the most strapping Brontë, Emily got to drag her sodden brother home from the Black Bull. Sylvia, attracted to men larger than she, took one look at the six-foot Ted Hughes at a Cambridge party and decided he was "huge enough" to interest.

As mature women they came across as self-absorbed, temperamental, prone to violent outbursts, a bit intense. They belittled and they mocked. "(H)alf amused and half in scorn" Emily listened to sister Charlotte read a review of *Wuthering Heights*. Sylvia's journals contained "nasty bits" about friends, rivals, lovers and family, deleted from the published version. Bored or irritated with the company, both turned testily silent, ignoring social protocol. Sylvia's glaring-eyed muteness unsettled Olwyn Hughes, her sister-in-law and one time literary executrix. The chaplain's wife in Brussels complained that Emily "hardly utter(ed) more than a monosyllable" when invited to her home. Neither seemed to put undue effort in playing nice—which makes the inclination to judge their work by that criterion all the odder.

Sylvia had "the rarity of being, in her work . . . never a 'nice' person," Elizabeth Hardwick noted in a *New York Review of Books* article. Her anger on the page, her appropriation of the Holocaust as personal symbol of oppression and what Olwyn Hughes called her "appalling vindictiveness" have all been criticized. To Aurelia Plath, her daughter's novel, *The Bell Jar*, represented "the basest ingratitude." In *Wuthering Heights*, Charlotte found "scenes which shock more than attract." To "strangers . . . unacquainted with the locality," the work "must appear a rude and strange production," she said, fretting elsewhere: "Whether it is right or advisable to create beings like Heathcliff, I do not know; I scarcely think it is."

Because *Wuthering Heights* was the first piece of literature I read, whenever I feel the urge to reread it, I suspect the drive of sentiment, that those critics who dismiss it as an overblown Gothic romance have a point. But only before I begin reading. Despite its doomed love theme and merging souls motif, *Wuthering Heights* is solidly a novel of revenge. The Catherine beloved by Heathcliff dies halfway through; the rest of the plot revolves around getting even, Heathcliff-style. Although emotions throughout are torrential, they're rarely rhapsodic. The author accepted a brutality in the human character that neither of her writing sisters, Charlotte nor Anne, could face without the balance of redeeming love, human or godly. Of the three, only Emily presented degradation, betrayal, greed and the struggle for power raw, without ruffles or flounces. Life could be dirty and ugly in Emily's canon, and death provided no redemption.

In Sylvia's "dawn poems in blood," as she called those final compositions before her suicide, she too dispensed with the ruffles and flounces. Using a lexicon of powerfully elemental images— blood, root, water, stone—she documented betrayal, revenge and an incendiary rage.

Neither wrote what the literary establishment of the time expected women to write. Once Emily emerged from the Ellis Bell nom-de-plume, critics speculated that her brother Branwell produced some, if not all, of *Wuthering Heights*, convinced no female would conjure the story on her own. In the introduction to Sylvia's *Collected Poems*, published in 1981, Ted Hughes admitted to excising the "more personally aggressive poems" of 1962 from the *Ariel* collection, setting off one of many controversies regarding destroyed and reordered manuscripts owned by the Plath estate. "How ironic," Marjorie Perloff remarked in *The American Poetry Review*, "that the publication of Plath's poems has depended, and continues to depend, on the very man who is, in one guise or another, their subject."

Emily's authorial choices were tampered with when Charlotte undertook "the sacred task" of republishing her sister's work in 1850. Eager to present Emily's contributions in what she considered the best possible light, Charlotte changed the punctuation, the paragraphing, the spelling and the dialect in *Wuthering Heights* and removed all Kingdom of Gondal references from the poetry.

If Emily and Sylvia wouldn't censor themselves, those who lived longer would perform the service for them.

Both tried, for a brief stretch, to teach. "Oh, only left to myself, what a poet I will flay myself into," Plath confided to her journal between grading papers at her alma mater, Smith College. Teaching exhausted her, and she bitterly resented the energy drain. Again and again she complained of feeling too tired to read, much less write. Emily preferred the house dog to her students at Law Hill and said so. Sylvia lasted a year at Smith, Emily a few months at Law Hill. Away from home, Emily turned morose and despondent, then physically ill. She preferred to live in Haworth, take care of the parsonage and her pets, wander the moors and write.

The highlight of the first floor of the Brontë Parsonage tour is the dining room where the sisters wrote. Engravings of Thackeray and the Duke of Wellington hang on the walls—Charlotte's heroes, not Emily's. The dining room also contains Emily's death bed, a sofa that looks uncomfortably short for a woman 5' 7".

Emily's bedroom upstairs contains no bed. After her death and Charlotte's marriage to the curate Arthur Nicholls, Charlotte enlarged the bedroom next door, reducing Emily's to closet size. Scarcely wider than its single window, the space is now furnished with nursery toys. As a little girl Emily slept, or tried to sleep, in a bed shoved next to the window with its view of wind, rain, the church graveyard, darkness and ghosts. She suffered terrible nightmares but turned those torments into poetry: "Sleep brings no rest to me;/The shadows of the dead/My waking eyes may never see/Surround my bed."

Biographers, straining to categorize, have decided that the creator of the salacious Heathcliff was a "sexless" creature herself or, more poetically, a "passionate celibate." Whatever her personal situation, Emily didn't have to look far to observe the lovelorn. Branwell pined for the married Mrs. Robinson, the mother of a former pupil; Charlotte pined for her (also) married teacher, Constantin Heger; Anne went doe-eyed at the sight of curate William Weightman. Surrounded by a suitor cast of refined teachers and curates, the sly and "sexless" Emily took out her pen and

created the rough and tumble Heathcliff, a brooder with a pronounced sexual pulse.

The building that inspired Wuthering Heights (the residence)
may or may not have been an abandoned farmhouse high on the
moors, but Top Withens is within striking distance of the museum
gift shop and accessible by hiking the Brontë Way. The path
through meadows and fields is also maintained by the Brontë
Society and, with the exception of sheep, lies deserted this day
because of the inclement weather. Stone fences dating from the
eighteenth century crisscross the fields. What looks to the modern
eye like natural beauty is actually a man-made phenomenon.
Large-scale tree clearance and animal grazing during the Bronze
Age created the moors, and continuous grazing combined with the
effects of a cooler, wetter climate keep them stark and foreboding.
    In 1956 Sylvia hiked to Top Withens while visiting her new in-
laws in Heptonstall. "The sky leans on me, me, the one upright/
among all horizontals," she wrote in the poem "Wuthering Heights."
    When you reach the top of the ridge, the sky does bear down
hard, but it's the wind that evokes Emily's text: a fierce, steady
buffeting that flattens heather and sways sheep.
    Emily isn't buried as she buried her character Catherine
Earnshaw amid the wild moors; she lies in the family vault below
St. Michael's. The closest you can get to her grave is a section of
stone flooring above it, several layers removed.

    "Dying/Is an art, like everything else," Sylvia wrote. She and
Emily were both more than a little in love with death. They made
its acquaintance early: Emily lost a mother and two sisters; Sylvia,
a father. Their attraction to death was physical as well as mysti-
cal. Visiting her father's grave in Winthrop, Massachusetts, Sylvia

yearned to "dig him up," to prove, incontrovertibly, his past exist-
ence as well as his death. In Emily's novel, Heathcliff twice digs
up Catherine, immediately after her burial and again eighteen
years later. Because of those postmortem investigations, he tells
the superstitious Nelly, the living stand "a better chance of keeping (him) underground."

Haunting by the dead was a given in *Wuthering Heights,* in
Emily's poetry and in Sylvia's. Disturbing, yes, but the visitations
also provided a certain amount of comfort, the last strand of connection between the living and the deceased. "You said I killed
you—haunt me, then!" Heathcliff begs the dead Catherine. The
dead in Sylvia's poem "All the Dead Dears" grip "through thin and
thick." As inheritor of his dead wife's literary estate, Ted Hughes
must traffic constantly with Sylvia's ghost. After Emily's death,
Charlotte wrote to her friend Ellen Nussey: "I cannot forget
Emily's death day; it becomes a more fixed—a darker, a more
frequently recurring idea in my mind. . . ."

A consumptive Emily caught cold at her brother's funeral and
died within weeks. Sylvia died after setting out milk for her sleeping children and sticking her head in an oven. Unlike 1953, when
she swallowed sleeping pills and curled up in the dirt beneath her
Wellesley home, in her London kitchen in 1963, Sylvia didn't rise,
Lady Lazarus-style, again.

Because she refused medical care and called the homeopathic
remedies passed along from W. S. Williams to Charlotte "quack-
ery," Emily also has been accused of a willful death. But why
should she have trusted medical miracles? She had watched her
mother, two sisters, aunt and brother expire in the care of expert
physicians, and her front yard was lined with soggy graves.

Few argue that Sylvia was mentally "well." Even the edited version of her journals portrays a woman battling deep, debilitating
depression. That Emily was a touch on the mad side, or headed
that way, has been argued by Muriel Spark in *The Essence of the*

Brontës. If consumption hadn't killed her, Spark speculated, Emily would have finished her life "mentally deranged." Since Emily remained workably sane until the end, why not the continuation of a routine built around tramping the moors, managing the family's railroad stock, mocking Charlotte's appetite for London literary society, writing more or writing nothing? Why not an eccentric, reclusive finale, but still a fate this side of crazed?

A public footpath runs from Hebden Bridge to Heptonstall, Sylvia's final resting place. Years ago one of the steeples of the town's parish church was struck by lightning and now sits on the ground, enshrined where it fell. The older the dead, the closer they huddle around the lightning-struck church beneath tilting tombstones decorated with lichen. The tombstones of Sylvia's circle, laid out in a newer cemetery across the road, are primarily granite. As a group they seem to hunker, less high than wide. The marker that reads Sylvia Plath Hughes squats near the front of the cemetery, within the '60s row, and although I have travelled a long way to find it, when I do, I feel a jolt.

Unlike Emily's, Sylvia's grave is totally accessible to the pilgrim. I can touch the headstone, the mud above the coffin, the thorns of the two permanent, straggly rose bushes growing on its mound. I can recite one or ten of her poems in homage, standing above sprigs of heather and berry branches and a single pink carnation wrapped in cellophane. Without the help of guidebooks or organized bus tours or bilingual signs, Sylvia's admirers have found this place.

People don't last, but a "good poem lasts," Esther Greenwood declared in *The Bell Jar.* A "good poem lasts a whole lot longer than a hundred . . . people put together."

If that statement weren't true, I wouldn't have crossed an ocean to stand beside a poet's grave.

Night
Life

In the money-lean years before the house expansion, when I slept in my parents' bedroom, packed in among their double bed, a chest of drawers and a vanity, my single bed was the piece of furniture farthest from the door, closest to the night. Afraid of that night, instead of waiting for natural closure, I squeezed my eyelids shut and prayed feverishly for morning.

Few country dogs die of old age. Before they can, most are finished off by trappers, hunters or cars. When my first rabbit dog disappeared, I was still too young to realize the consistency of that rule and expected her safe and sound return. I watched "Lassie"; I read animal books; I trusted in that kind of fairy tale. I hoped she would arrive by day, but just in case she chose night I kept watch from my bed, searching for a wagging tail. With a mission I felt less afraid of peering at the moon-splotched yard and driveway. Hope blocked terror, and because I anticipated my dog, not a monster, gradually I grew bolder, extending my lookout to the edge of the woods. I suppose it was inevitable that one night I'd conjure her image, a pale and shimmery version of her former self. I rubbed my eyes, believing and disbelieving in that apparition, trying hard through force of will to convert her to her old substantial self. When that effort failed and continued to fail, I came to accept the alteration, working out an explanation that consoled. My pet might be dead, but she wasn't gone. As a ghost dog, she could still, on occasion, return home to visit.

Watching and waiting for those impromptu visits, I made peace with the mysterious outside and the shadows that dwelt there. Unhappily for me, that victory didn't eliminate my night terror altogether. As soon as the exterior threat subsided, interior spooks took up the fright slack. A trio of witches, icy and vindictive, held court from the vanity's mirror, standing between me and light and my parents' comforting presence. For all my newfound courage, I couldn't consciously cross their path. To escape my bed and the bedroom, I had to sleepwalk.

At first I padded to the living room where my parents watched television, circling that space with ritualistic precision, they reported. Later I ventured farther—into the kitchen and outdoors. Once I walked through a string of mud puddles, climbed into our Ford, placed one hand on the steering wheel and the other on the ignition switch. (In Shawboro, back then, people left keys in cars.) What saved me from zooming off down the field path was the idea that Mom should come along.

In her dreams she heard me calling, she said. A plaintive summons, almost a wail. After searching the house, she ran outside to find me sitting, waiting, hands in the ready position.

She must not have screamed. She says she asked what I was doing.

"Going for a ride," I answered.

"Wait till morning," she advised.

In the neighborhood, I wasn't the only kid who sleepwalked. Clark Brinkley lived in a huge two-story house at the very center of Shawboro, a house that once belonged to my great aunt Hattie. Twice a week or so Clark climbed out his top floor bedroom window and strolled around the porch roof until he slipped and fell into the shrubbery below.

I dreamed less during my sleepwalking stage, but my anxious mother dreamed more. At breakfast she regularly alluded to troubled REM's, withholding the specifics.

"Just bad," she'd say. And if I pressed for more: "I don't know. Just bad."

But she did know, every one of those disturbing images burned into her brain, she simply spared me their haunting. She probably assumed I'd appropriate her horrors, weaving them into my own midnight dramas. She was probably right.

I only remember Dubby sharing one of his dreams at breakfast or at any other hour of the day. In it, his father floated above the bed. They talked—Dubby staring upward, Jack circling the ceiling. After a miserable, protracted dying, the dream Jack seemed jovial, released, and to see him that way reassured my father. It wasn't a nightmare; it was a pleasant encounter.

Hearing the plot, my mother and I exchanged glances—happy for Dubby's sake, but envious. Why didn't we rate pleasant, reassuring dreams?

The first year of school desegregation in Currituck County, I had a string of "mediator" dreams. Wildly agitated, I rushed back and forth between groups, black to white, white to black, urging peace and conciliation on all fronts and earning everyone's unmitigated contempt.

In college my roommate and I kept dream logs for a psychology course. The night I starred as a New York heroin addict, she lay on a doctor's table, giving blood. When dream soldiers accosted her behind a classroom building, French snipers fired on me as I crawled through the brush. The morning I described my Pennsylvania boyfriend zooming through telephone wires and coalescing in our apartment, she yelped: "No! You didn't!" Finally, we had a match. She'd also dreamed David had been transported by telephone.

Under a Freudian spell, we read and reread *The Interpretation of Dreams*, fascinated by the lead-off example in chapter eight. A grieving father falls asleep in the room next to his son's corpse, a corpse surrounded by lighted candles. He dreams his dead child shakes him awake, infuriated by his negligence. The candles are burning him. Doesn't the father realize the candles are burning him?

The classic anxiety, the father/son dialogue, not even the resurrection theme interested us as much as the juxtaposition of that dark, sleeping chamber and the freakishly lit chamber of the dead. The shadow-play between those two connected, disconnected rooms must have been awesome, we thought. Awesome and mesmerizing.

If I'd still trusted Freud when I dreamed my slew of dead-and-in-the-coffin dreams, I might have gleaned solace, some hint of continuity, in his claim that all dream journeys are reminders of death. My funeral dream sequences were elaborately staged, protracted miseries of confinement. I dwelt obsessively and claustrophobically on my too tiny coffin. Trapped inside, when the family's tears dripped on my skull, I screamed that I was alive, but no one paid attention, closing the lid and burying me anyway.

If I'd bounced from Freud to Jung, his one-time apostle, I might have recognized the next group of dreams I recorded for the escape strategies they were.

Dreams, Jung proposed, revealed not only what the dreamer desired, but also what she needed.

September 3:

X and I are in bed. A noise wakes me. I discover a couple chatting above us. The girl is short, midget-like; the man is very tall. X converses complacently, unsuspiciously, with them. But I'm nervous. Both the back and front doors are locked. How did they get in?

December 16:

Hundreds of people, myself included, on a cliff's edge. There are two distinct choices: climb down a steep ladder or lunge down a steep bank. All around me people are choosing and acting to save themselves. I stand paralyzed.

December 17:

On a train with X. My suitcase and clothes are strewn about; I'm desperately trying to merge them. Switch to evacuating class-room, the bell ringing. I'm completely panicked, but still attempting to pack.

December 18:

With many suitcases and female friends, rushing to the airport, away from X's house, I keep falling asleep. My friends have to handle all the details.

Athens, May 22:

A nude woman tortures herself with hot irons and knives. As if in a documentary, the question: **Why is she doing this?** *(Many women in the city are torturing themselves for unknown reasons.) After each branding, she looks with terror toward the corner before resuming. I follow her gaze. A man. Immediately identifiable as a hypnotist. It's suddenly clear he's the one forcing women to kill themselves. He asks if there's a Taurus in the room. People turn and stare. "You are mistaken," I say. "I'm an Aquarius." "What is your name?" he asks. "Kathy Russell," I lie. He leaves, but, on the street, on my parked car, I find a slip of paper that reads:* **Kathy Russell's hand involuntarily jumped when I mentioned Taurus.**

May 28:

I'm dressed in a black tutu. A fake ballerina. Initially I'm dressed in a white outfit, but my dresser understood by grunts that I preferred the black. A knock on the door—my costar in black also. He wears a cowboy hat with veil. He smiles; I smile. Apparently we've been waiting for this, our big scene, a long time. He ties the bow around my neck with his teeth—for effect. For effect, I scream mercilessly. He hoists me onto his shoulder, runs. While playing dead, I try to assist. In the darkness we aim for a cover of weeds, dive in, disappear, but our disappearance is unsuccessful. We're found.

I didn't escape X in dreams when I escaped him in life. He continued to reincarnate in the guise of a Bram Stokeresque vampire, complete with black cape. Whenever he intruded on the dreamscape, he startled me, then vanished. Even in dream-time calculations, he never tarried. The night I skied fast and furiously down a white slope, exhilarated by the speed and freedom of that run, at the bottom of the hill he stepped from behind a tree and directly into my path. Then he raised his cape/wings, extending the blockage.

"I'll get you for this," he announced.

After which, poof, he disappeared.

The Macedonians believed nightmares could be discouraged by eating parsley, wild carrots and the black seeds of male peonies. They also believed shaving the head, inflicting tiny slashes in the throat and bleeding the ankles worked as deterrents. By bleeding myself, I might have avoided a vampire's bloodletting—an extreme method of prevention, but isn't the symmetry engaging?

Still, of all dream theories, I preferred the incubus/succubus explanation. I liked the idea of a beast squatting on my chest, manufacturing my dreams. A wild and unruly animal, maybe, but immortal and therefore reliable. A dog-like pet you could count on to find its way home night after night.

Recently I've been dreaming about excrement: wads of it underfoot or dive-bombing the air. A good omen, according to the Assyrians. In their dream book, feces symbolize wealth. Twentieth century interpretations aren't quite so upbeat; they regard the image as evidence of an arrested ego and foolish, childish defiance.

As a class, female nightmare sufferers harbor doubts about their true worth, Ernest Hartman informed the afflicted and the general public in 1979. His studies, he said, showed such a group to be inordinately suspicious and distrustful—people who, by and large, felt totally incapable of getting through the everyday. Many, many women for many, many reasons have difficulty navigating the everyday. And if they succeed, their reward is the booby prize of night. Night and its henchman, the nightmare.

As an adult, I banned mirrors from my bedroom—not to avoid witches, I've dealt with witch fear, but to avoid my own night image, shadow-crossed and sleep-distorted. I've been told I laugh aloud in my sleep nowadays: a laugh that's not totally a laugh, rather an eerie, slow-speed A HA HA HA, an outburst that sounds more strained than gleeful. I can't say I'm surprised. Mirror-free, I'm still waiting for my batch of pleasant dreams, still struggling to believe all is well in a pitch black room, still yearning to become a grown-up version of the lucky ones who figured out how to side-step fright without walking in their sleep.

The
Piracy of
Acquaintance

In the maid's quarters of a faded pink motel, the occupant of room 217, a repeat customer, was the focus of endless rumors and innuendoes. Cora the laundress and Abigail the head housekeeper were long-time motel employees, hired before the pink began to fade. Each had an opinion on the mental health of resident 217.

"She's been crazy as a loon as long as she's been coming here," Abigail said.

"That's not so," disputed Cora. "Every year she's gotten worse."

"How long has she been coming?" I asked.

"Ten years," Cora said.

"Twelve at least," said Abigail.

"I'd bet money on ten," Cora insisted.

Abigail scoffed. "Twelve if a day."

The Dunes wasn't a chic motel. Vacationers chose it because of its location near the beach or because they appreciated its funky, vintage qualities. From a distance it looked wind-whipped. Up close it looked the same.

I cleaned, tidied and vacuumed room 217 and several other second floor efficiencies, free after 1 P.M. to do as I pleased. The job was low stress, part time, menial and very productive. Scouring a rank bathtub, dumping trash and untangling twisted sheets can impart a true feeling of accomplishment—basic but satisfying. Another plus: the work allowed me to snoop with impunity. Pajamas, brands of toothpaste, medications, paperbacks, the scent a room takes on after a night with its tenant(s) all provided clues to the lives within—relatively nondescript lives until resident 217 arrived.

When I knocked the first morning on her door, I interrupted a conversation carried on by two versions of the same voice. Neither responded to my greeting.

The next morning, on orders from Abigail and Cora, I knocked longer and harder.

"She's had those sheets for two nights. If you don't get them today, I'll never get them clean," Cora fretted.

Someone crept heavily to the other side of the division and waited as I waited. I felt my cheeks go chipmunk through a keyhole lens. I held high my supply of soaps, cleansers and matches to appear official. I also coughed.

Day Four, Abigail turned threatening. If the sheets didn't get in by my hand, she'd stuff the damn things under the door herself.

"I'm leaving some fresh towels and things. Out here. On the floor," I called in sections, then moved noisily on to room 219. I bumped the vacuum cleaner against the baseboard, turned on the bathroom spigot, turned it off and strained to hear the twist of a doorknob. Eventually a chubby, many-ringed, liver-spotted hand with severely bitten fingernails snatched the clean bundle and replaced it with a urine-scented wad.

According to Cora and Abigail, wealthy relatives paid for resident 217's vacations, provided they were distant. She took almost all of her meals in her room, but when she ordered in the motel's restaurant, the waiters and busboys heard various personalities arguing over the menu. Five years before, the manager of the Dunes had begun discreetly adding a laundry surcharge to her bill, which was discreetly paid. There had been worse guests by far.

In time I got her to open the door wide enough to pass through the towels and sheets. She was a short, stout woman who wore her gray-streaked hair in a long ponytail. Her smile, outlined by red lipstick, was skittish; her eyes, as best I could tell in the shadow of the door, hazel. Either handing over the fresh linens or receiving the soiled bunch she pushed back, I smiled steadily, trying my best to look absolutely guileless, absolutely harmless.

But resident 217 was wise to keep that door wedged between us. I wasn't harmless, not entirely. The moment I became intrigued with her story I became a kind of menace. She might have been crazy, resident 217, but she wasn't stupid. She suspected the ingratiating maid before her desired to spy as well as serve, and in that presumption she was one hundred percent correct.

I didn't need to spy on John Cloud. He was a man only too happy to divulge his intimacies. According to him, intimacies were the product of an uptight world. He had no secrets. Secrets "inhibited."

John Cloud, in an orange Datsun pickup filled with jars of organic fruit juice, picked me up on Interstate 84 near Hartford because he rescued all hitchers, he said, regardless of talent.

From New York he was heading home to Vermont, "the real interior." In two months he'd sold five new clients on his label.

There was a shitload of money to be made in the health food business, he declared. If only he'd realized the depth of the market earlier, he could have dropped out of the "computer game" and New York long before.

"You won't stay in New York either," he predicted with confidence. "New Yorkers don't see. They look at you but they don't see."

To demonstrate that flaw, he turned his wide smile on the occupants of a passing Oldsmobile, Empire State plates. The driver ignored him, but the kid in the back seat waved.

Nope, I was no New Yorker, John Cloud assessed, and certainly no hitcher. Sagging shoulders, an apologetic offering of the thumb, frantic motion of any kind marked the novice. The professional, on the other hand, radiated a mixture of assurance and belligerence. Driver selected, establish eye contact. Then concentrate: totally. Command attention, never beg. Stranded for three days in the deserts of Utah, no car in sight, John Cloud focused his energies on producing a vehicle. When it appeared, driven by a woman partial to the '60s rebel look, she invited him to her ranch for two weeks of R & R.

"I've never been passed by a woman, not once," he gloated.

So who had passed him by? I asked.

The occasional husband and wife team; male bureaucrats.

"Loners freak out company guys. With them it comes down to a real battle of wills. My force, their resistance. But I've won more than my share."

When our paths diverged at Interstate 91, John Cloud invited me to visit his "space of peace" north of Brattleboro.

"You're out of New York—it's a done deal," he said, smiling his bully smile.

Before he drove off, I asked one more question: his real name, the one that preceded the invention.

For a millisecond the bully smile disappeared.

Because I had a wimpy thumb, the hitching guru assumed I was everywhere wimpy. Far less savvy than resident 217, John Cloud thought by telling his story his way I would hear it his way. Whatever he assumed, once he gabbed, John Cloud's story belonged to me.

I wasn't hitching when I met the driver of a blue Buick in Macon, twenty-odd miles short of Interstate 85 in North Carolina; I was having car trouble. Between the Dismal Swamp and Norlina, where State Road 158 connects with the interstate, Carolina terrain is flat, gray farmland, dotted with small communities and the rare gas station. On a two-lane road surrounded by uninhabited scrub pine, I passed the Buick a mile or so before the alternator light on my dash flared red.

I kept driving—I didn't have much choice—until I reached a country store with gas pumps. As soon as I lifted the hood, the problem became apparent: a broken fan belt. It would have been a minor mechanical mishap if that mishap hadn't occurred in Macon after 5 P.M. The Buick had also stopped at the country store, and its driver promptly joined me, commiserating as I stared at the frayed, useless belt. He mentioned a full-service Texaco station "down the road a bit," and suggested I get in his car and let him drive me there.

I didn't remember a Texaco station in the vicinity, and I'd driven the route many, many times.

"Thanks, anyway," I said, hoping to sound casual. "I think I'll just call a mechanic from here."

When I closed the hood and walked back toward my purse, he walked with me, a forty-five-ish, lacquer-haired man whose fortunes showed too clearly in his polyester suit, tight in the shoulder, short in the leg. From his wallet he pulled a photograph of his family, pointed out a daughter "around my age." As further proof of his good character, I suppose, he offered a soiled business card.

"I appreciate the offer," I lied, "but I might as well wait for the mechanic."

He, too, waited while I went inside and dialed the number of the only mechanic the proprietor "could think of, right off the bat, who might come out at this hour." In a nearby rocking chair, her husband made a meal of orange sherbet, sucking the plastic spoon.

"If he didn't have any cars to work on at his shop, Gene might have gone home early," the proprietor said as the number rang and rang.

Next I tried the sheriff.

"I expect the sheriff's having supper this time of day," she said.

When I dialed the highway patrol, the dispatcher advised me to try the local sheriff, a local mechanic.

I looked outside. The Buick was still there, its patient driver leaning against it.

"It's just that I'm a little nervous, travelling alone," I admitted to the woman fanning herself with a newspaper.

"Well, we close in less than an hour. I suppose you can keep trying to find someone till then."

"You're lucky you caught me," the mechanic said when he arrived in the dim twilight. "I was about to go out for the evening, and that would have been a mess for you."

Yes, that would have been a mess for me, I agreed, watching the Buick leave at last.

"I don't mean to scare you, but out-of-town cars parked here overnight tend to get their tires slashed. Fact is, these days I won't let my wife drive anywhere alone. You just don't know about people anymore. You sure don't."

The mechanic's paranoia doesn't entirely convince me mine was justified or that, in my zeal to read situation as narrative, I didn't malign a perfectly decent Samaritan. I sometimes wonder which is more dastardly: to write about the known or the unknown? Should I put to paper the schoolmate who embezzled, served her sentence and made news again as Avon's leading sales rep, or opt for a stranger glimpsed once in the yellow light of a Madrid train station? Whether I pick and choose the details or invent them whole cloth, I distort the story, mold it to my purposes. Either way, I take what isn't freely given.

To justify the shady business of telling tales, for a time I stuck these quotes on the bulletin board above my desk:

"If you write all about anyone they do not exist anymore for you and so why see them again?"—Gertrude Stein

"[A] biography is considered complete if it merely accounts for six or seven selves, whereas a person may well have as many (as one) thousand."—Virginia Woolf

"Lack of conscience makes a person healthy, take it from me."—Heinrich Boll

"I decided I was a very stupid fool not to at least paint as I wanted to when I painted, as that seemed to be the only thing I could do that did not concern anybody but me."—Georgia O'Keeffe

Another story, then.

The persons involved will take issue with tone, pacing, content, dialogue and more. They will say it didn't happen this way, that it happened another way or that it never happened at all. But they aren't the author; they aren't me. And once I write out this version, no other will ever again seem nearly as true.

So:

In a banquet/seminar room of a New York City Holiday Inn, the three of us who arrived together sat thirteen rows back from the podium—I counted. The predominately beige room accommodated a fully beige audience. The most caustic of our trio had already offended the welcoming committee by refusing a name tag. The second indifferently pasted his ID to the company brochure and left it there. Only I displayed mine where the welcoming committee wanted it displayed: between my collarbone and left nipple. Unless or until someone stole my notes, I intended to behave amiably.

The evening's moderator, neatly dressed and brown-eyed, introduced himself as a one-time lower-level executive and many-time bastard. He acknowledged the scattered applause with a smile, perfectly at ease with the label because, as he explained, it belonged to a time long past. Gravely, no smiles now, he declared that he had "amended" his personality and "powered away" all former mishaps and mistakes.

Again the audience applauded.

Other testimonials followed.

A highly agitated, red-faced man had learned to "love indiscriminately"; another, once "embarrassed to be," had "eliminated all barriers to his being." The grade "A" had been "pulled" from a professor's head. A love relationship had turned into "white light." A woman from the front row raised her hand to share the experience of tracking down a cabby she'd stiffed—not to give him his tip, but to let him know she knew she'd added no gratuity, thereby "completing their relationship."

Ernie, twenty-six, a lapsed Catholic, an attractive man with broad shoulders and large hands, the man who invited his college buddies and me, the tagalong, to this event, wanted us to explore with him what we had seen and heard and felt in the upstairs seminar room downstairs in the bar. He was anxious; he was solicitous; he was hopeful as he quietly declared his love for all of us—even for me, the tagalong he barely knew.

He was told to cut the crap. Friends were friends.

Ernie sadly shook his head. Not so long ago he'd been a complete wreck, he said.

"Everyone's a wreck."

But again Ernie shook his head.

In addition to the crew at our table, there were two other sets of drinkers and a piano player who wasn't drinking but probably should have been. She sang badly and had trouble keeping up with herself on the keyboard. It was difficult to use her performance as a diversion, but the three of us tried before Ernie's brother, fresh from an upstairs sensitivity session, walked in. In passing, he applauded the singer mid-song. She nodded in his direction.

"See," he announced. "Everyone craves reinforcement."

According to Ernie's brother we were, at the very moment he spoke, embroiled in a revolution of mammoth proportion. One that would, among other improvements, eliminate subway filth.

Our Mr. Caustic, quickest on the draw, said he "loved" subway filth. Adored the stuff.

Ernie's brother turned huffy.

"Either you're part of the revolution or you aren't. Either way, the revolution continues."

"Fuck the revolution."

There passed a moment of unclaimed silence. Ernie looked crestfallen.

His brother, after a beat, demanded we explain our "hostility. I want to understand your viewpoint," he said. "I really want to hear where you're coming from."

We doubted he really wanted to hear all that.

"But I do," he persisted. "I really want to dialogue."

It wasn't much of a dialogue. We called him a shithead, said his idea of utopia sucked, and the shithead smirked grandly.

Only Ernie accompanied us through the vacuumed lobby out to the filthy street. Twice more he thanked us for coming. He really appreciated the effort, he said. Our participation meant a lot to him. MY attendance and participation meant a lot to him, he said.

And as he said it, meaning it, I mind-travelled to that immaculate penal colony where the desire for acceptance and approval from anyone and everyone had wiped out every other scruffy, seditious desire.

It's an image I recall whenever I begin to brood too long and hard on the ethics of telling tales.

Collecting
Postcards

For five full minutes one spring in a crowded post office, I watched a man stand next to the out-of-town drop slot and with extreme caution, extreme deliberation, lift postcards from a fat stack and edge each one toward the free-fall that represented, in the great mail universe, the first of the journey from here to there. He must have held thirty postcards—the tan, pictureless kind sold at the counter. Even so, he treated each with reverential importance. None of the frenzied surrounding activity affected his methodicalness or his concentration. If other harried correspondents, irked by his non-speed, brushed past and commandeered the chute, he didn't object. Wherever they had intervened in his arc of movement, for him, time stopped, and he held that position—hand on stack or card in midair—waiting with pronounced languor for the interruption to pass. Then, once again, at his own inimitable and uninfluenceable pace, he resumed his mission.

He took almost as long getting a postcard through the opening as he took getting it from pile to slot. First he balanced, then once, twice, three times, delicately tapped until it dropped. After each send-off, he slowly, slowly, withdrew his finger and slowly, slowly, examined and reexamined its tip. With each card he followed exactly the same procedure, and then he and his tapping finger ambled out.

If a person devoted that much time to the mailing, how many hours had he spent penning the actual communiqués? And what about the content of those dispatches to the outer world? Vernal greetings or suicidal ravings? The tan, bland, official rectangles offered no clues. If only he'd opted for picture postcards, so much more would have been revealed (intentionally or unintentionally). The picture can sub for the message; quite often, the image says it all.

I started collecting picture postcards because they were cheap souvenirs. For fifty cents or less, a tourist can possess an exact replica of the surroundings without the camera hassles. With postcards you don't have to worry about the quality of the light, the direction of the sun or f-stops. You're guaranteed a professional angle on the territory, a clear-cut rendition of its charms. Close to home and farther away, I bought postcards at gas stations, grocery stores, gift shops, hotel lobbies, flea markets and vegetable stands—wherever postcards were sold, I bought.

I didn't limit my collection to bridges (Brooklyn, Golden Gate) or skylines (St. Louis, Miami) or fog (Mendocino, Provincetown). I didn't favor bars or beaches or mountains or pumpkin fields. I was catholic in my tastes for lay-of-the-land scenes, and soon I branched out to include state-of-mind evocations as well. A man staring dementedly through venetian blinds. A child in bloomers and sun hat, looking lost against a great tank of ocean. An androgynous form wrapped in bed sheets, reclining above the caption: "She couldn't sleep unless she was thoroughly tucked in." I chose that sleeper card for the shroud, the snubbing of claustrophobia and the heroic if senseless assumption that mere cloth could shield the world of dreams from black and white reality.

I bought postcards to remind myself of a certain scent (daffodils), a certain temperature (the White Mountains in January) and particular atmospheric conditions—humidity (a healthy stand of kudzu) and aridity (the massive salt flats of Death Valley).

For a while I collected disaster and disaster-in-the-making panoramas: the San Francisco earthquake, 1906; an atomic test site at Yucca Flat, Nevada, 1953. Then I moved on to movie stills— a plump and tremulous Judy Garland accosted by Margaret Hamilton's witchy fingernail. Briefly, too, I gathered literary and political celebrities. Che with cigar, Djuna with pearls, Gertrude with poodle. But the features of the famous absorbed too much of my attention. My gaze invariably locked onto their overexposed mugs, shunning the broader setting.

The same law applied, and applies, to family albums. Paging through, in search of an erstwhile fence or grapevine, I become distracted, then riveted, by the relatives junking up the scenery. Postcards or photographs, past and present, my response is the same. If the nose, eyebrow or cheekbone looks familiar, no natural wonder, not even Niagara Falls, diverts me. I continually align with the human scale.

In the process of collecting, I filled several boxes and then another several with postcards. An overload. Carting them from one apartment to the next began to seem increasingly silly and finally counterproductive. The sheer bulk of the accumulation worked against my original purpose. I'd wanted the postcards to serve as memory prompters, associative flash cards. Thumbing through hundreds felt closer to memory burn-out.

My collection mania ended with a postcard of a boarded-up

summer house on the Yucatan Peninsula. The house, called El Pastel, sat across from the malecón. It had been photographed showing a porch, a patch of street, and palm trees fore and aft. Walking along the beach, with a bit of effort, the tourist could zero in on the exact location of the photo shoot, as I did on several occasions, holding up a copy to the genuine article and waiting for some kind of convergence.

Never happened, of course. The palm trees had grown, the wind direction had changed, more paint had worn off the shutters and dropped to the sand. If I'd made a career of standing on that beach, gazing for the remainder of my days, I wouldn't have matched the reality of El Pastel with its *tarjeta postal.*

An obvious conclusion, you might say. Once the careful mailer of postcards had tapped his last missive through the slot, the exhibition was over; that moment, like every other, swallowed by history, certifiably unrecoverable. Too true. And yet the uniqueness of that gone-forever tag might have increased the value of my postcard collection. The singularity of the vanished moment might have caused me to prize my stash all the more.

Instead, I grew alarmed.

Somewhere along the line a preference, and a scary one, had slipped in and established itself. My attachment to and affection for realism had become way too extreme. I had begun to worship exclusively at literalism's shrine, shortchanging the powers of abstraction and metaphor, confusing perfection with persuasion. When it happened, where it happened, exactly how it happened, I wasn't sure, but the fallacy had definitely taken root.

Worse was still to come. On that Yucatan beach, treating one image taken by one camera during one moment in time as the truer, more authentic rendering simply by being the stuff of postcards, I caught myself acting as if imagination didn't exist.

The

Farm

Scamp, scoundrel or neither, my grandfather purchased 72 acres of cleared land, 109 acres of woodland and 14 acres of worthless swamp in Crawford Township, Currituck County, North Carolina in 1915. Portions of that plat had been part of "the John Sears plantation," circa 1835. The farmhouse that came with the property in 1915 didn't come close to plantation-grade; it was merely a livable house—four rooms, two upstairs and two down, fastened together with wooden pegs and insulated by shredded newspaper. By the time Jack and Dora took possession, John Sears and the Civil War had come and gone, and the war that raged in Europe. Farmers fought the only timeless battle: digging into the soil, enticing it to produce—which it did, some years better than others.

My grandfather worked the land with a hand-steered plow hooked to a mule, and he picked cotton by hand, a cotton sack looped around his neck. In a photograph of him, surrounded by acres of cotton bolls, his wild white hair matches his crop.

"Cotton was a big crop at that time. The money crop," James Ferebee says, a farmer Dubby's age who knows about money and how to make it. Like Dubby, he also started farming with his father, but James Ferebee is an expansionist by nature. These days he oversees the only farming business in Shawboro large enough to legitimately qualify as an agribusiness, and he continues to diversify, planting broccoli and other crops uncommon to the area. James began with a few men, but his current payroll is extensive. While I was in high school, Dubby hired a man who lived near Indiantown to help him in the fields—a one-shot deal. He didn't like the responsibility of employees, he said, but I believe the plainer truth was he liked to farm alone. I wasn't born early enough to witness the pre-tractor days of my grandfather, but I remember watching my father on his first John Deere, disking row after row of his mama's acres under a blue sky and looking nothing less than a contented man.

As a newly married addition to the family and a new set of hands, my mother was expected to pick cotton in her father-in-law's fields.

"Hard work, the hardest, picking cotton," she says. "All that bending over."

Primed to encounter a coiled copperhead every step of the way, she wasn't the smoothest picker, but no one could fault her agility. Any movement beneath the leaves sent her leaping up and back, way back, out of a nipper's striking zone.

As a cash crop in Currituck, cotton fizzled even before my grandfather died. In the forties, with enlistees off to another war and home folks signed up for defense work in Norfolk, too few were available to pick cotton. The crops, locals say, rotted in the fields.

My brother started working in the fields with Dubby as an adolescent and continued as long as he lived at home. Craig dug miles of drains by hand, just his muscles and the flat dull blade of a shovel to propel the dirt. Sometimes I'd trudge through the mud or dust to deliver a tomato sandwich and a jar of iced tea, and he would take a break, evaluating his progress.

"Almost finished," he'd optimistically conclude.

I agreed to be encouraging, to be companionable, but squinting toward the unfinished direction, I usually thought the stretch between us and the woods seemed a considerable distance, a lot of hand-blistering shoveling to go.

Occasionally during the drain digging but more often during disking, arrowheads and bits of pottery churned to the surface. Craig's collection, carefully preserved in a cigar box, included brown, burnt orange and off-white spears, and one smooth gray ax weighing in at five pounds. Craig used to line them up on his bed in order of size, and we'd stand back, amazed by the fact that what lay before us had been carved by Indian tribes who called home the same stretch of land the Meads tribe called home. We're still amazed to this day. Holding an arrowhead is an exercise in confronting mortality. In the big scheme of things, humans are the elements that come and go.

On maps or from the air, the farm resembles a horseshoe, fitted into and around acreage owned by other Shawboro transplants or heirs. My grandfather's deed, preserved on Virginia-Carolina Joint Stock Land Bank letterhead, meticulously outlines the boundaries and ownership rights on all sides. Solid ground rims the north, south and west ranges, but the east is lined by The Great Swamp, close cousin and neighbor to the more poetically named Great Dismal. When William Byrd of Virginia arrived in 1728 to settle the state line dispute between Virginia and North Carolina, the swamp's yellow flies, chiggers, ticks and cottonmouths disgusted his surveying team. "A dismal place," Byrd carped. The swamp that edges the farm shares many of the Dismal's beauties and varmints. The expanse is filled with white cedar, black gum, cypress and red maple trees; loons, herons and egrets; vultures and red-tailed hawks; mourning doves, whippoor-wills and screech-owls; black bears, bobcats and foxes; cotton-mouths, copperheads, and enough frogs, lizards and toads to marshal a plague. When my father was a child and when I was a child, on summer nights the swamp croaked and hooted and sang us to sleep.

Pre-automobile, the dirt road laid out between the swamp and the sycamores in my grandparents' yard served as the main buggy track from lower Currituck to Shawboro and Elizabeth City. During my brother's Boy Scout days, his troop frequently camped on a patch of flat, level ground adjacent to the then-unused and over-grown route. The section of woods on either side was especially pretty and filled with hardwoods. In the winter, red-berried holly bushes broke up the brown and gray palette. Getting to that Eden posed problems, however. Troop members had to cross several deep ditches on slippery, decomposing logs, and overloaded back-packs, clumsiness or simple terror toppled more than a few. Dry-ing out by campfire was unadulterated drudgery, slow and tedious. I know because when Dubby took his turn as scout leader, I tagged along to share the ditch crossings, the dry-outs, the tent set-ups and the suppers of underdone chicken and overdone marshmal-lows. The moment the sun disappeared, the ghost stories began. In darkness, it scarcely mattered how close we camped to Dora's house. We huddled in a spooky woods that muffled screams and stayed black, deep black, until morning.

The safest time to tromp through the woods, fields and ditches is winter when the ground cover has died back a bit and you can, for the most part, navigate without tripping over tangled vines or disturbing anything that bites. In recent years, rather than settle in for an overfed snooze after our Thanksgiving feast, Dubby, Craig and I walk the property with the dogs and usually the cat but seldom with Mom. We take off down the field path behind our house and circle the old barns Jack built for his mules, plows and blacksmith tools.

If my father planted winter wheat, there's the thrill of that green wash in the pale light, and if we're lucky a deer or two will bound across the cut in front of us, aiming for the woods, oblivious to our presence and for the moment hunter-safe. Despite the no trespassing/no hunting signs that ring the property, hunters are everywhere, not all of them accurate shots. Neither Craig nor Dubby hunt anymore, but when they did, my mother cooked what they killed—squirrels and rabbits, mostly—and we ate that game, tough or tender. It was a free meal. Craig stopped hunting more or less when Dubby stopped, and one day Dubby just stopped. Times weren't that desperate anymore; we could afford to buy our suppers, and he preferred walking the woods to shooting.

When these fields aren't planted in wheat, they're planted in soybeans or corn. Dubby has never tried potatoes or peanuts. During good years, those crops deliver a higher profit margin, but they're riskier. For any healthy yield, farmers depend on moderate weather: sun, but not too much; rain, but not too much. With potatoes and peanuts, the dependency increases. A relentlessly dry or rainy spring will make any farmer brood, but potato and peanut farmers are especially vulnerable because the seedlings of those crops rarely recover from deprivation or excess.

By late May or early June of any given year, Shawboro's corn crop starts to tassel. For me, as a kid, tasseling corn meant corncob dolls and I took to the fields, searching for the fullest, longest, reddest tassel: my doll-to-be's head hair. A stiff wire shoved through the cob, snowman-style, passed for arms; a few crayon smears marked the eyes, nose and mouth. Corncob dolls were fun, but you had to play long and hard with your doll of choice its first day of creation because the tasseled hair shriveled overnight. Nothing practical or magical could restore it to its former beauty. When the season's first doll lost her charm, a lot of my friends opted for replacements. The switching felt too callous to me. Each corn season I allowed myself one doll and one only, which guaranteed a brief, intense bonding. Day Two I conducted a solemn funeral service, buried her dry husk and left a wreath of pine cones to mark the hallowed spot.

Although I buried my corncob dolls hither and yon, the farm hosts a more organized graveyard for dogs, at the first field curve, beneath apple trees planted by Uncle Carl. Two of my beloved Labradors lie there and other canines fed and loved by my cousins. There is also a human graveyard near the edge of the woods across from the second field cut, but winter or summer those graves are hard to see, thorn-wrapped and neglected and ever-sinking. No Meads bones rot there. Supposedly it is the resting place of several members of the John Sears family. The names, if ever there were names inscribed on the tilted, moss-covered headstones, are illegible and have been for a very long time, eroded by the years and the elements. By now the bones beneath those markers are so ancient even the dogs race indifferently over them, no scent left to sniff.

As soon as we veer away from the woods, we hear less hunter gunfire, more dirt bike roar. Silent moments are precious few. The local kids ride in packs, Dubby says, along a ten-mile, well-marked course that weaves in and out of Shawboro. Farmers' kids nowadays learn to drive dirt bikes, then graduate to tractors. Hailing from an earlier generation, my brother first learned to drive a John Deere. The girl child, I learned to drive my father's turquoise pickup. I'd practiced with Dubby in the cab, but I'd never driven solo until the day came when he needed to leave the tractor in the field overnight and told me, at lunch, to collect him near dusk. I think I screamed I was so excited. My mother, both alarmed and annoyed, said:

"She's too young, Dubby."

I was eleven—practically grown! But I avoided the "practically grown" argument; that tack had failed me before. Instead I latched onto the distance issue, as in: no distance at all.

Dubby backed me up.

"It's not that far, Ann," he calmly said. He said everything calmly.

In the meantime I had yanked her over to the window.

"You'll be able to see the truck the whole way," I pleaded.

"Not the whole way," she corrected.

"She can do it," Dubby said. Meaning: she's able.

Capitulating, my mother pressed hard against her temples, trying to box off another migraine in the making.

However long I was supposed to wait before setting off, I rushed the deadline. That rutty field path subbed as my Autobahn. I tried my best to hit third gear before reaching the dog graveyard, and once past that marker, I floored the accelerator, clutched the steering wheel and bounced up and down like a jack in the box. At the back cut, I stomped the brakes, jumped out in a cloud of dust, waved triumphantly in Dubby's direction and jumped back in, psyched for the joyride back. Once we did return, unscathed and in one piece, my mother burst into tears from the sheer strain of imagining me flipped over in a ditch full of red bellies.

"Aw, Ann," Dubby said.

She said: "I can't help it."

Neither could I. From that point forward, I wanted to drive incessantly.

A few years after my initial run, my younger cousin Carl Lee trashed the same pickup on the third curve, the sharpest turn for tractors or trucks.

"Said he got his foot caught," Dubby says, laughing as we pass the crash site. "Said he couldn't get it off the accelerator."

Reminded of that excuse, Craig and I laugh too, knowing Carl Lee's foot wasn't the only thing that got caught. Before he took that hairpin curve, every atom in him was consumed with the desire to conquer at maximal speed.

By the time Carl Lee had wedged the pickup in one of those red-belly infested ditches my mother so feared, both the snakes and snapping turtles that once thrived in that ecosystem had thinned out considerably. In their heyday, some of the snappers grew a foot long, not counting their tails. My brother taught me the evil trick of stick goading. Sufficiently goaded, a snapper locked onto its torturing device and resolutely held on. If your arm and stick were strong enough, you could lift the amphibian out of the water and sometimes entirely clear of the ditch. But once those jaws snapped open, you had to scat.

When hog farming became the rage, the run-off from the enterprise filled the ditches that fed into the swamp, Meads ditches included. That sludge ended the reign of the snapping turtle and depleted other forms of wildlife, including muskrats and minks and otters, once plentiful enough to trap. My grandfather trapped and my father trapped and my brother trapped. In the winter before breakfast and again just before sundown, Craig trudged off in his insulated underwear and hip boots, breath icy in the air, to check his set. He didn't always come back with a mink or an otter, but he usually came back with several muskrat pelts to sell for a couple of bucks each to the furrier, J. J. Flora, in Moyock. With Craig's generation the tradition ended. Whatever their feelings about the practice, pro or con, our youngest cousins can't trap; there simply aren't enough animals left to catch.

The ditch next to the property line we share with James Ferebee used to supply the best pelts. Even today the bank of that ditch offers us the best view of Shawboro proper—the farmhouse once owned by Colonel Henry Shaw, seed of the Shawboro name; the post office; Providence Baptist Church; the railroad tracks; and the grain bins where Dubby sells his corn, wheat and soybeans. For a moment, coats turned up against the wind, we take in the vista, Dubby pointing out the additions and expansions; then we turn south and eventually east to enter a stand of woods where Craig once talked of building a house when he talked of coming home and farming with Dubby. A lovely notion but unrealistic. There isn't enough land to support two families; there never was.

My family's farm is a small farm, fast becoming a relic, and my father's breed, the small farmer, is headed for extinction as surely as the snapping turtle. Ten years from now neither small farms nor small farmers will exist. Economics won't permit the aberration. Already farms up and down Currituck County are being subdivided into lots and sold to the spill-over of metropolitan Norfolk. At most that commute is a forty-minute drive.

Every time I walk this circuit, I wonder how much longer what I see will remain what I remember, unspoiled and intact. The land will outlast the Meadses, every one of us, but during my own lifetime I very selfishly and self-servingly want the farm to remain the farm I know and love. Its dependable stasis is a large part of what frees me to wander elsewhere. Coming back and checking in enables me to check out. Without these acres and these roots, vegetative and familial, I'm not sure I'd find the vagrant life quite so appealing. Without a firm base, I might find flitting to and fro more wearying than invigorating, a sad and aimless pastime, a drain on the body and the spirit.

As the dogs rush ahead of us toward a grove of leafless maples, Dubby stops and examines a patch of ground the falling leaves have missed. The prints are fresh and huge: unmistakably bear tracks. After a long hiatus, the black bear population is once again on the rise. From his back porch, Uncle Carl saw a mother and cub frolicking last week.

"These woods used to be full of black bears," Dubby says as we reach the dirt road once travelled by Jack, Dora and their wagonload of children, on the eve of turning a Sears outpost into a Meads compound.

It's a clear, bracing day; it's Thanksgiving. I'm walking family land with family. I know I should feel grateful for various sparings and resurgences—the bears have staged a comeback; the farm has survived another year—and I do. But with regard to the farm, disappointment is inevitable. Preservation of this place isn't impossible, but, increasingly, preservation is unlikely. Already alterations have occurred, some subtle, some startling. I have to come to terms with the irrevocable fact of change and accept in my heart what I already know in my head: that a fact will run roughshod over preference and sentiment every time.